The church has been self-diagnosed with gospel malnutrition in recent years. The remedy for such a condition is a clear and canonical articulation of the gospel – the message of 'good news' revealed throughout Scripture. In *Always Good News*, Scott Lothery gives the contemporary body of Christ the kind of supplement it requires by explaining not only what is good about the gospel, but how it is good. By summarizing the gospel with the Bible's orderly emphasis of Lord–Sin–Savior–Faith and contextualizing it with personal and powerful examples and analogies, this book shepherds the Christian toward daily spiritual health.

EDWARD W. KLINK III, Ph.D.
Senior Pastor, Hope Evangelical Free Church, Roscoe, Illinois
Professor, Trinity Evangelical Divinity School, Deerfield, Illinois

After the past few years, we could all use some good news. The good news about good news is that we know the gospel of Jesus Christ gives the ultimate, best news to a broken world. But more than that, the church's call to share this good news is more urgent than ever. That's why I'm glad Scott Lothery wrote this book. It offers practical, clear wisdom on the message and the mission we have from God.

ED STETZER, Ph.D.
Executive Director of the Wheaton College Billy Graham Center and professor and dean of the Litfin School of Mission, Ministry, and Leadership at Wheaton College

An incredibly striking book, which revealed to me how I had imperceptibly 'slipped' into wrong thinking about sin, suffering, the Lordship of Jesus, God's love and my expectations of Christian discipleship. I wholeheartedly recommend it as a spring clean to make sure you are living and breathing the right gospel.

RICO TICE
Senior Minister at All Souls Church, Langham Place,
Author and Founder of Christianity Explored Ministries

We all need to hear more good news – and that's why you'll want to keep Scott Lothery's book close at hand. It will remind you of the greatest good news the world has ever heard: the gospel of Jesus Christ. I have personally benefitted from Scott's teaching on the gospel (which is the same teaching as the Bible) throughout the years, and I trust you will too. Tell it to your own heart. Share it with others. This is the good news we are most desperate to hear and believe every single day.

KRISTEN WETHERELL
Author of *Humble Moms, Fight Your Fears*,
and co-author of *Hope When It Hurts*

Many categories that contribute to forming the heart of the gospel run counter to the way most people, whether Christian or not, think today. Therefore, it is not surprising that people find it difficult to accurately describe the message of Jesus. This little book engagingly describes the meaning of the gospel of Jesus as found in the Bible and helps us to come to a fuller, richer understanding of it. The book ends with a provocative, yet persuasive, discussion on why using the word 'love' may not be the best way to summarise the gospel. I recommend this book for new and mature Christians and for others interested in finding out what Christianity is all about.

AJITH FERNANDO
Teaching Director, Youth for Christ, Sri Lanka
Author, *Discipling in a Multicultural World*

This book is a gem! Whether a person yet to discover the greatest news ever to reach our planet, or one who has received and believed it, yet in need of recapturing the wonder – this is for you. Scott Lothery masterfully unfolds the good news of Jesus Christ in such a way that it will bubble in your heart and overflow through your lips. Always the best form of evangelism.

MIKE MELLOR
Evangelist and Author

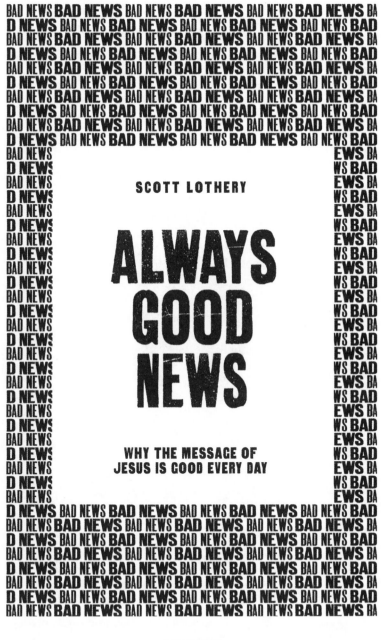

SCOTT LOTHERY

ALWAYS GOOD NEWS

WHY THE MESSAGE OF
JESUS IS GOOD EVERY DAY

CHRISTIAN
FOCUS

Copyright © Scott Lothery 2023

paperback ISBN 978-1-5271-0969-8
ebook ISBN 978-1-5271-1021-2

10 9 8 7 6 5 4 3 2 1

Published in 2023
by
Christian Focus Publications Ltd,
Geanies House, Fearn, Ross-shire,
IV20 1TW, Great Britain.

www.christianfocus.com

Cover design by
Nate Baron

Printed by Bell & Bain, Glasgow

CONTENTS

To my beloved wife Cindy,
You are always good news in my life!

Introduction

* * *

WE live in a bad news world, don't we? Every morning when I wake up, I'm in the habit of taking a brief look at an app on my iPhone to check out the world headlines. I also like to relax with my wife in front of the TV each evening to watch a broadcast of what's happening locally. In both cases, the reports are overwhelmingly negative. There are probably studies that have analyzed the ratio of bad news to good news, but anecdotally to me, it feels like it is 10:1. It's relentless.

Some people have suggested the reason for this disparity is simply emphasis. That is, news organizations are businesses. Businesses need to make money. And bad news sells much better than good news. Thus, the media emphasizes bad news.

There's definitely some truth to that point of view. In a 2014 study, the web recommendation platform Outbrain discovered that negative words are 30 percent more effective at catching our attention than positive ones and negative headlines increase the click rate of smartphone users by 63 percent. Other research has provided similar data. There's no question that consumers prefer bad news. It's one reason the media majors on it.

But I think there's more to it than simply businesses giving the people what they want. We live in a bad news world, not just because of the emphasis of the reporting. We live in a bad news world because there's actually more bad news than good news to report. Good certainly happens, but the bad is always right there with it and clearly seems to outweigh the good.

For example, I'm not sure there is a more joyful occasion than a baby being born. I love when I am at a hospital and Brahms' lullaby is played over the loudspeaker to celebrate a birth. Some veteran labor and delivery nurses say it still gives them a warm feeling every time. It brightens their day and never gets old.

Yet, some people hear that lullaby and are filled with grief because they haven't been able to conceive a child they desperately want, or because their last pregnancy ended in miscarriage, or because they experienced the horrifying loss of a still birth or an infant mortality. The song that is designed to bring happiness to all who hear it has the opposite effect on them. It's only a reminder of their deep pain.

But even if we are among those who smile ear to ear when we hear that tune and think only about the wonder of a newborn child, that delight doesn't last that long. It's fleeting. It's here one minute and gone the next. Why? I think it's because deep down we all know that all births eventually end in the ultimate sadness of death. The grave casts a foreboding shadow over every umbilical cord that is cut. Nobody who comes out of the womb can avoid the tomb. The sting of death always pierces through the joys of life. No matter how good the good is, the bad is always right there with it.

Every birth ends in death, every loving relationship has conflict, every healthy body gives way to decay, every family knows the pain of disease or disability, every country suffers disasters, and every well-designed plan is disrupted by something that goes wrong. Every single time something good happens, it seems there is a 'yeah that is good, but …' moment that follows at some point. That's not pessimism. That's just reality. Bad news always looms on the horizon of life.

We live in a bad news world because the bad outweighs the good. Evil is alive and well on planet Earth. Look at these headlines from just a single day through a simple internet search:

- 'Spat Ends in Murder' – A painter was murdered by his friend when he refused to treat the latter to a drink on a Sunday evening at the bar.

- 'Twisted Cleric' – A former Ukrainian monk-in-training pled guilty to killing a thirty-nine-year-old nun at the religious academy.

- 'Mom Help Me!' – A twenty-year-old woman helped her twenty-five-year-old boyfriend cover up his murder of her twenty-month-old daughter.

- 'Where Were the Adults?' – A teenage boy was charged with homicide after deliberately suffocating his four-month-old nephew.

This is one day of news just on the topic of murder. A man killing another man over not picking up the tab. A monk killing a nun. A young mother protecting her boyfriend even after he killed her daughter. A boy killing a baby. Evil is alive and well on planet Earth. It is in every segment of society in every part of the world.

We live in a bad news world because there's actually more bad news than good news to report.

I don't know about you, but sometimes I get discouraged by the headlines I read on my iPhone. I get disturbed by the prevalence of evil I see in the news on TV. I get anxious about the bad things that happen in my life. And I am often troubled by the sinful tendencies I find lurking in my own heart. I suspect your experience is the same.

We all need to hear more good news! And not just temporary good news like a Brahms' lullaby that makes us feel good for a moment or a day or two. We need much more than uplifting words that ultimately get dampened by the onslaught of bad news. We need a daily dose of good news that both transcends all the bad news and puts every bit of it in a hope-filled framework.

So, I wrote this little book for you to know that type of news exists. It really does! Historically, it's called the Gospel of Jesus. This message about Jesus of Nazareth is so good that it warrants being heard and shared every day. It's good for me. It's good for you. It's good for everyone. It's so good that no bad news can bring it down. It is able to respond to every 'yeah that is good, but ...' moment with, 'yeah that is bad, but ...' perspective. It's always good news.

My heartfelt prayer for everyone who reads this book is to know this good news about Jesus so well that you can easily bring it to your mind for the good of your own soul or quickly speak it to others for their encouragement. You are going to want to remind yourself of it every day. And you are going to want to share it with others.

1

The Subject of the Good News: Jesus of Nazareth

✳ ✳ ✳

GENDER reveal parties are all the rage these days. If you aren't familiar with this event, it is a gathering of family and friends usually held during the second trimester of a woman's pregnancy to reveal a baby's sex. Sometimes even the parents themselves don't know if they are having a boy or a girl prior to the occasion as the sonogram results are kept a secret by one person who is in charge of the reveal. It can truly be a surprise to every guest except one.

Apparently, parties like this began as recently as 2008 when a married couple who were really excited about their first child decided to have a cake with pink frosting in the middle as a way to announce to their guests, 'It's a girl!' Since then, people have smashed pinatas, popped balloons, set off fireworks, and even brought in a live ultrasound technician. Google the topic and you will find plenty of over-the-top examples.

And though there is always the potential for a curmudgeon to be disappointed by the reveal, these are happy occasions. Even if you want the baby to be a boy, it is good news to find out it is a baby girl, and vice versa. New life is worthy of celebration. That's why we have birthday parties every year.

When our four children were born, we had the technology to find out if they were a boy or a girl, but the tradition at that time was simply to do birth announcements. The most common way to tell people the good news about your new baby was to send out a postcard in the mail with a picture of him or her. Creative types who wanted to do more than that would put a stork on their lawn in blue or pink with the baby's name on it.

It's hard to know exactly what kind of birth announcements were common in ancient times, but we know for sure that one birth had a very uncommon announcement – Jesus of Nazareth. His gender wasn't revealed at a party. His arrival wasn't declared through the mail or on the front lawn of his home. It was heralded by angels. Look at the way an angel announced the good news about Jesus' birth to some shepherds out in a field, keeping watch over their flock by night ...

'And the angel said to them, "Fear not, for behold, I bring you good news of great joy that will be for all the people. For unto you is born this day in the city of David a Savior, who is Christ the Lord."' Luke 2:10-11

This announcement is fascinating and wonderful, but it does require some explanation to understand what the angel pronounced that day around 2000 years ago and why it is so relevant and good for us today.

First and foremost, notice the news is about Jesus of Nazareth. I will address the declarations about him being the Lord, the Christ, and the Savior later in this book, but for now, it is important to linger on the simpler observation that Jesus is the subject of the angel's announcement. The good news is about him. He is the focus.

In other words, the good news doesn't begin with 'God created the world,' and continue with, 'You are a sinner,' because the focus of the message isn't what God did all the way back when time began, and it certainly isn't about you.

Articulating the news in that way is a bit like being in charge of a gender reveal party and making it about the guests, the parents and all the lineage of the child from ancestry.com; or sending out a birth announcement that portrays family and friends as prominently as the baby and even has a little mirror in the corner so that you can take a glance at yourself while looking at the photo.

While its true that the scope of Jesus' *impact* on history, theology, cultures, nations, societies, individual lives, and civilization itself, is extremely *broad*, we must not let that cause us to lose focus on the fact that the scope of the *subject* of the good news about him is exceptionally *narrow*. It's *about him*! Jesus is not simply the hero of a long and complicated human story or the third act in a four-part play. He is the consuming emphasis of every bit of a specific proclamation from God called the Gospel. He is on the front page, the back page, and every page in between.

If someone asks me what the good news about Jesus is, the first word of response out of my mouth is 'Jesus' because the content of the message inescapably revolves around him. He is the subject of the news, its constricted center. Therefore, he must be the subject of the sentences we use to communicate the headlines about him. That's the first point to notice about the angel's announcement.

Second then, notice another obvious but sometimes overlooked point. The angel said the announcement is good news. News – that's its genre of communication. This is really crucial. It's not an op-ed, an advice column, a worldview, a vision for life, our actions, or a fanciful story. It's objectively true and vitally important information about Jesus that has eternal significance for all humanity. It is news, and it is oh so good. It's always good news.

That's what the etymology of the *Koine* Greek New Testament word *'euangelion'* suggests. That is the root of the word in Luke 2:10 that is translated into English as 'good news.' The prefix *'eu-'* refers to something that is good or pleasant. The root *'angelion'* is the word for 'message.' The combination of those terms would lead us to believe it is a 'good message.'

A simple etymological analysis alone can be misleading though. For, while a 'racecar' is, in fact, a car that races, a 'butterfly' is not a fly that butters your toast in the morning. Right? We must do more than analyze the components of a word to determine its meaning. We must also analyze how the word was used in its original context.

In the case of *'euangelion,'* it was often used in the first century to announce a great military victory but could also be used simply to celebrate more common events. For example, when Caesar Augustus eventually emerged as the Roman Emperor out of the turmoil resulting from his adoptive father Julius Caesar's assassination, his ascension to the throne was announced across the Empire as the *'euangelion'* of Caesar Augustus. At the same time, a person who recovered from an injury could spread that *'euangelion'* to their friends and family. The semantic range of the word indicates that it was used to communicate good news of all sorts.

Think about the last bit of good news you received. The CT scan shows no cancer! You got the job! You are going to be a grandparent! The school of your dreams accepted you with a full scholarship! The angel described Jesus' birth as this kind of good news, but even better. It wasn't the typical kind of good news. It was a unique form of *'euangelion,'* a bit more like the *'euangelion'* of Caesar Augustus than that of someone recovering from an injury, but even more special, even more important, even more profound, and even more relevant to everyone.

Further, notice this news is packed with exceedingly great delight for 'all the people,' not just some of the people. The news is SO good. And it is SO good for everyone. In other words, the news isn't restricted in its goodness by wealth or social status. Rich, poor, and middle class are all invited to hear it and celebrate.

The message isn't limited in its goodness by ethnicity. Praise God! Mongolians and Mexicans, Africans and Australians, Inuits and Incas, are all encouraged to listen and rejoice. The announcement isn't confined in its goodness by age or sex. Male and female, children, teenagers, young adults, middle-aged, and the elderly are all welcomed to pay attention and applaud.

The proclamation is not constrained in its goodness to people with specific physical characteristics or social interests. Tall and short, thin and portly, muscular and puny, beautiful and less than attractive; those who like sports or band camp, theater or robotics club, politics or helping at the soup kitchen, books in the study or a hike in woods; everyone is urged to delight in what is said.

And perhaps most amazing of all, the news is fantastic for everyone no matter their religion or philosophy or morality. The righteous and the wicked, the spiritual and the secular, the pagans and the pious are all summoned by God to stand up and cheer.

Don't miss this important theological description of what is historically referred to as the Gospel. The intention of God in the person and work of Jesus of Nazareth is for the good of all humanity, our great joy in fact. The message was announced back then and is still announced today so that everyone celebrates.

Now, if you have haven't heard this news before in the way that a cancer patient would hear the news about a clean CT scan or someone unemployed would receive news about being offered a great job, you simply must keep reading. If you haven't felt comfortable sharing the Gospel with someone else like you would tell them you just became a grandparent for the first time or the school of your dreams was giving you a full ride, don't put this book down.

I'm going to share some things with you that you may have never heard before, but they come right out of the Bible. You do not want to miss them. The Gospel is the best news of all time. And it is for all the people, meaning it is good for you every day.

2

Jesus is the Lord

✳   ✳   ✳

PACIFIC Garden Mission has a wonderful legacy of over 150 years of compassionate service to the homeless in Chicago. And they are so bold about the good news of Jesus and its central place in this mission. I love their signage. They have one that says, 'Christ died for our sins.' My favorite, though, is their iconic cross. Have you seen it? It has the word 'Jesus' on the horizontal beam and the word 'Saves' on the vertical beam starting from the middle 's' in Jesus. Everyone who drives by that bright neon sign gets the message – Jesus saves. That is a key part of the Gospel and probably what is most often associated with Jesus, even by many non-Christians. He is the Savior.

As much as I like that sign though, the Bible indicates that the word we should most associate with Jesus is not 'Savior,' but 'Lord.' When we think of the good news about him, we should first think about his Lordship. Jesus *is* the Savior. That's true. We should certainly believe that and teach that and celebrate that. No doubt about it. Pacific Garden Mission should be admired for proclaiming it twenty-four hours each day in neon lights. Yet, according to the Scriptures, the word that we should prioritize in our description of him – like if we had to choose just one word – is the word 'Lord.'

In our modern language, if we want to emphasize a word, we use punctuation like an exclamation point, change the format of the text to italics or all caps, or simply underline it. In the days that the Bible was written, those word processing tools weren't available to the authors. So, they used repetition. If you wanted to emphasize a word, one way you could do that was to repeat it.

Did you know the word 'Lord' is the most frequently repeated *noun* and the 14th most frequently repeated *word* in the entire Bible – almost 8,000 times? That is a lot of repetition. The word occurs more than they, be, is, not, him, them, it, with, all, thou, was, and thy. The Lord is the overwhelming emphasis of the Scriptures.

Furthermore, 'Jesus is the Lord' is the primary focus of the New Testament. How do we know that? Consider the frequency with which the two words 'Lord' and 'Savior' occur alongside the word 'Jesus.' That simple analysis is one way to determine what is stressed about him and it is quite revealing. Whereas the words 'Jesus' and 'Savior' appear exclusively just eight times in the same sentence, the words 'Jesus' and 'Lord' appear 163 times in that way. That is a huge difference. It's about a 20:1 ratio of independent occurrences of the words. Jesus is the Lord is emphasized much more than Jesus is the Savior.

To get that data to soak into your brain, try the following auditory exercise. I want you to put this book down in a minute and say some phrases out loud. Humor me. It will be helpful to you. Hopefully, you are alone as you probably don't want to do it in a coffee shop. Start by saying 'Jesus is the Lord' twenty times. If you are like me, you will have to count it out on your fingers. Then, say, 'Jesus is the Savior' once. Then, do both again for a total of forty-two statements spoken aloud. Ready? Go for it!

How did it sound? You just did a verbal demonstration of the data regarding those words in the New Testament. If you are curious, here's what that data looks like in print: Jesus is the Lord. Jesus is the Savior. Jesus is the Lord. Jesus is the Savior.

For as much as people think of Jesus as the Savior, and rightly so, we must all multiply those thoughts by twenty in thinking about Jesus as the Lord to be thinking biblically. That's the emphasis of the New Testament and it is the first part of the good news. When preaching in the ancient city of Caesarea, the Apostle Peter said:

'As for the word that he sent to Israel, preaching good news of peace through Jesus Christ, <u>he is Lord of all</u>.' Acts 10:36

The Gospel begins with that simple announcement – **Jesus is the Lord**. That's the first headline. Although that is a straightforward statement, it has deep meaning and profound implications. There is more to be discovered in the articles of this frontpage story. What did the Apostles mean when they proclaimed Jesus as the Lord? And why is that always good news?

Well, they meant that his Lordship is comprehensive, perfect, and permanent. Let's spend a bit of time exploring each one and reflecting on why each one is good, not just for the Apostles 2000 years ago, but for us today as well. First, Jesus is the Lord, that is, he is the King. He has comprehensive authority over all things.

The King

The most life-shaping experience of my childhood was when my sister Jody was diagnosed with cancer, slowly emaciated over several years as she battled the dreadful disease, and then died in our home on December 7th, 1984. The last nine months of her life were especially cruel to her, but also did significant collateral damage to me.

Since my room was down the hall from hers, I had no choice but to pass by it every morning and every evening. Obviously, I wanted to be there for her as she struggled, but at the same time, I was just a teenager trying to deal with what was happening. A periodic break or rest from the trauma would have been one coping mechanism, but it just wasn't available to me. Death had sort of a personified presence among us that was inescapable, and I could never get any relief from its relentless pursuit of her. Day after day after day, I watched as she gradually slipped away from this life into death's horrific grip.

Sometimes the nights were worse. Not only was my room down the hall, but it was also adjacent to hers. The headboards of our beds bumped up against the wall that our rooms shared which meant that less than a foot of dry wall separated us when we slept. I can still hear her cries of pain on the worst of all nights. That marks you for life. For several years afterwards, the unnerving voice of death lingered as an indelible impression on my soul. I heard it consistently whispering to me, 'I am coming for you too.'

While it was all very emotionally disturbing, it also made reality crystal clear. Through my sister, I learned firsthand that death oversees humanity. It is ruling. Everyone will eventually succumb to its power, no matter how strong a fight they put up. It reigns as king, and everyone must bow the knee to it at some point. Death is the Lord of all. That was the lesson of my teenage years.

You can imagine, then, how wonderful it was for me to hear the Gospel of Jesus during college. I still remember that initial feeling of joy and hope as I heard the good news about the One who had more power than the power that took my sister.

I didn't believe it at first. It just all sounded too good to be true. But, after some research, I concluded that the resurrection of Jesus of Nazareth is well supported by the evidence of history. He really did walk out of that garden tomb. The stone was actually rolled away. He truly overcame the grave.

Even more, his resurrection was followed by his ascension to the throne of the universe. That's what the Bible teaches. He beat death and has been installed as the King over everything. As the Apostle Paul clearly stated:

'For God has put all things in subjection under his feet.'
1 Corinthians 15:27

In other words, all the types of power known to humanity are subject to him – spiritual, political, economic, cosmic, military, natural, etc. The good news is, no matter how it may appear, death is not in charge.

I still hold tightly to that truth every single day, not just for my sister, but for everyone I know who has faced death. Every time that I hear about someone dying, I think, 'That's bad news, but Jesus is the Lord over even death.' His authority is always good news in this way. It puts the worst news in a hope-filled perspective.

And it's not just that death is not in charge. Neither are wicked dictators, natural disasters, oppressive bosses, debilitating disorders, greedy billionaires, demonic forces, worldwide pandemics, abusive parents, unjust systems, or compulsive behaviors. All these authorities are vastly inferior to him. He is far above, and they are far below. Nothing is left out of his reign, and no one can rival his rule.

Jesus is the Lord, that is, he is the King. He has comprehensive authority over all things. That's the first Gospel aspect of his Lordship to celebrate as good news. The second is his perfection. He is the Christ.

The Christ

Up until the 1980s, Superman was the best-selling character in American comic book history. His widespread appeal was not simply because of his unprecedented powers. Sure, superhuman strength is awesome, X-ray vision is fascinating, and enhanced hearing is handy. Furthermore, who does not want to be able to fly.

Yet, those extraordinary abilities alone are not what won the hearts and minds of readers. Superman is beloved in the American culture even today primarily because of his virtue. He is a super-*hero* with an unwavering commitment to the welfare of humanity. He is all about justice, righteousness, kindness, and bravery. He is the perfect combination of power and goodness.

That is why it was always good news to the regular folks when they heard he was coming to town. It meant he was going to vanquish the evil that was oppressing them. Would Superman's arrival on the scene of trouble always be greeted with joy if he had a flawed character or a moody disposition or situational ethics? Of course not. We love him because he is good inside.

Such it is with Jesus Christ. Someone could argue that having comprehensive authority over all things as the King is not necessarily good news. After all, the question remains … what kind of person is he and, thus, how is he going to use that power? Well, you'll be glad to know that Jesus is not merely good inside. He is flawless. Moreover, his perfection is for your good. And it is described in that word 'Christ.'

When I was a kid, I thought Christ was Jesus' last name, and, well, a cuss word too. When I became a Christian, I discovered it was a title that meant 'anointed one.' The Hebrew Bible prophesied that a man would be born anointed from God, perfect in all his ways. He would come to his people Israel as the promised Messiah to fulfill the covenant God made with them; all the moral, civil, and ceremonial aspects of it. He would be the true Israel, who embodied all God called Israel to be. Where that ancient nation failed to live according to God's ways, the anointed one would succeed. Jesus is that man, the Christ. That's why the Apostle Matthew records him as having said:

'Do not think that I have come to abolish the Law or the Prophets; I have not come to abolish them but to fulfill them.'
Matthew 5:17

Perhaps a way to say this in our contemporary terms is that Jesus is the only human being who has ever lived in right relationship with God in every way. Everything he thought was right. Everything he desired was right. Every attitude he had was right. Everything he said was right. Everything he did was right. He was tempted in every way humanity can be tempted, yet, unlike the rest of humanity, he never sinned against God. He is the perfect human being.

Isn't that amazing news? There is someone in charge of this world and the person in charge is thoroughly good inside. In other words, wicked dictators, natural disasters, oppressive bosses, debilitating diseases, greedy billionaires, demonic forces, world-wide pandemics, abusive parents, unjust systems, compulsive behaviors and even death itself are not in charge. The one in charge, Jesus, is displeased with all of them, because they do not reflect his goodness to the world.

He tangibly demonstrated that displeasure in his earthly life – even proved it – when he did things like healing the paralytic in Capernaum, calming the storm on the Sea of Galilee, driving a legion of demons out of the man from the Gerasenes, raising Jairus' daughter from the dead, and inspiring the tax collector Zaccheus to give half his riches to the poor and return defrauded money fourfold. Whatever suffering you may encounter in this world, you can be confident and rejoice in this good news: Jesus is not happy about the situation either, because he is good, and he wants his goodness spread to everyone.

When the Apostles proclaimed, 'Jesus is the Lord,' they first and foremost meant he is the King. He has comprehensive authority over all things. It was about his position. Secondly, they also meant

Jesus is the Christ. He is perfect in all his ways. It was about his person. The final aspect of the Lordship of Jesus that is good news is his permanence. He is the Son.

The Son

Though American culture increasingly views Christianity as negative, even immoral, it is not uncommon for non-Christians to have a positive view of Jesus of Nazareth. For example, Muslims celebrate him as an important prophet. He is the most referenced person in the Quran, receiving 187 mentions. Similarly, Hindus regard him as an insightful life instructor. In a 1926 letter to Milton Newberry Frantz, Mahatma Gandhi wrote, 'Jesus was one of the great teachers of mankind.' And in 1996, the Dalai Lama thought so much of Jesus that he wrote a book on how a Buddhist should appreciate his lessons.

Even many non-religious people esteem Jesus. Consider the atheist author Kurt Vonnegut. To the graduates of Agnes Scott College at their commencement in 1999, he said, 'Jesus of Nazareth told us to say these twelve words when we prayed: "Forgive us our trespasses as we forgive those who trespass against us ..." And for those twelve words alone, he deserves to be called "the Prince of Peace."' Throughout history, Jesus has been beloved by people of all kinds as a human prophet, teacher, counselor, and peacemaker.

Yet, as wonderful as it is to be admired, these views of Jesus are in direct contradiction to his own words. The fact of the matter is he did not view himself as merely a human being. He clearly claimed to be the Son of God. For example, consider the time when he was debating some of the Jewish religious establishment recorded in

John 8. They were arguing with him and brought up Abraham to which he replied:

'Truly, truly I say to you, before Abraham was, I am.' John 8:58

What a fascinating statement! Notice, he did not say, 'Before Abraham was born, I lived,' as if he was some sort of time traveler. No. He used the present tense to describe his experience of being alive prior to Abraham's birth. It was a grammatical reference to his eternality.

Furthermore, he used the designation 'I am,' because that is exactly the way God described himself when he spoke to Moses from the burning bush, recorded in Exodus 3:14. Jesus told them he was God in the flesh.

As a result, the religious leaders did what you would expect them to do given what they believed. They picked up stones to put him to death for blasphemy. It was obvious to them that he was committing a crime worthy of capital punishment in their society – equating himself with their God, Yahweh.

Isn't it odd, then, that his claim to be the Son is not obvious to everyone else who reads these accounts of his life in the Bible? It is so strange that, in a 2020 theological survey, 52 percent of American adults, including 30 percent of Evangelicals, indicated that they think Jesus was a great teacher but that he is not God, the Son. That's bizarre because no matter how highly a person thinks of Jesus, the idea that he is merely a human being is antithetical to what he said about himself. Denying his divinity is telling him he isn't who he claims to be. Why would anyone who does that call themselves his followers?

In *Mere Christianity*, C. S. Lewis explains this incongruence well. Lewis wrote, 'I am trying here to prevent anyone saying the

JESUS IS THE LORD

really foolish thing that people often say about him: I'm ready to accept Jesus as a great moral teacher, but I don't accept his claim to be God. That is the one thing we must not say. A man who was merely a man and said the sort of things Jesus said would not be a great moral teacher. He would either be a lunatic – on the level with the man who says he is a poached egg – or else he would be the Devil of Hell. You must make your choice. Either this man was, and is, the Son of God, or else a madman or something worse. You can shut him up for a fool, you can spit at him and kill him as a demon or you can fall at his feet and call him Lord and God, but let us not come with any patronizing nonsense about his being a great human teacher. He has not left that open to us.'[1]

Jesus claimed to be the Son of God. He is human, for sure, but he is more than human. He is a different category of being altogether. In the epistle to the Colossians, the Apostle Paul described Jesus as 'the image of the invisible God.' The author of Hebrews pronounced God's 'Son' as 'the radiance of the glory of God and the exact imprint of his nature.' The Nicene Creed teaches that Jesus is 'begotten not made' and 'of one substance with the Father.' The Apostle Thomas summed up all these ideas quite succinctly when he cried out simply, 'My Lord and my God,' after he touched the resurrected Christ.

The Gospel includes this declaration about the Lordship of Jesus, that he is the Son, and this declaration is indeed good news. Why is it so wonderful? Well, think about it. Jesus is the King means that evil is not in charge. No matter how it appears, not even death has the ultimate say. Jesus is the Christ means that he is clearly

---

1. C. S. Lewis, *Mere Christianity* (HarperCollins, 2001), 52.

dissatisfied with the current state of affairs. This world is a far cry from a reflection of his goodness.

And since Jesus is also the Son – a permanent and flawless King – surely, he must have a plan to right all that is wrong. A perfect God-man with all authority in Heaven and on Earth isn't going to sit idly by as his universe wallows in corruption. The Apostles knew that to be true. They experienced a taste of it first-hand. That is what they proclaimed as the Gospel of Jesus.

Imagine that someone is going to ask you tomorrow what the Gospel is and you want to get this straight in your mind now so that you will be able to answer them clearly and succinctly. Start with the word 'Jesus' because it is good news about him. That must be the first word out of your mouth.

Continue with 'is the Lord,' because that it is the first point the Apostles emphasized. That's the first headline. You don't necessarily need to drill down into the depths of his Lordship as King, Christ, and Son, but some of it might be helpful to your listener. Remember that simplicity and clarity is a priority over depth. Don't confuse yourself or them with all the Gospel's profundities. Emphasize Jesus is the Lord because that's always good news.

Then, tell them the second part of the message – Jesus, this one true Lord of the world, does have a plan … He is putting the world right regarding sin. You may wonder how in the world sin is in any way part of the good news. Or you may have been misinformed that sin is the bad news that has to precede the good news so that you know how good the good news is.

Well, be sure to read the next chapter to discover the truth that there is good news about sin. It's part of the Gospel.

3

Jesus is Putting the World Right Regarding Sin

✳ ✳ ✳

DURING the awful worldwide pandemic of 2019–2022, my wife and I started a very good habit of walking every night after dinner. It has been a great way to get a bit of exercise and reconnect after a busy day at work. Cindy is a registered nurse who works at a facility that was caring for people of all ages infected with the virus. Even after her long, hard days, she is always up for a stroll.

One evening, on the way down Princeton Avenue, she turned to me and said, 'Well, I have some good news and some bad news. Which one do you want to hear first?' I pondered for a minute and decided that I needed to hear an encouraging word before another undesirable one. I don't think 2020 was a good year for anyone. Like everyone else, I was fatigued from the relentless onslaught of bad news.

'Give me the positive first,' I replied. She said, 'The good news is that I am down to only five Covid-19 patients.' My wife is a saint of a woman, one of the front-line heroes in the fight against that dreadful disease. She regularly cared for fifteen to twenty people afflicted with it. As the person who loves her most in the world, this change was very good news. Though I was extremely proud of her sacrifices, I was also anxious for her to be out of harm's way.

'That is very good news,' I said, 'so what is the bad news?' She responded, 'Well, my boss told me we are no longer going to receive hazard pay.' About a month after infected patients filled up her unit, she received a bump up in her hourly wage. As much as it was helpful to get a little extra money, the bad news of that loss was significantly overwhelmed with the good news of her being on the trajectory towards safety in her job. So, my strategy of hearing the good news first worked perfectly. The bad news didn't bother me at all.

But it turns out that the order I picked isn't the order most folks prefer. Recent studies indicate that most people want to hear the bad news first. There seems to be some sort of psychology to it. It is probably why we usually serve our children a delicious dessert only after they have eaten their spinach. Apparently, human beings do not mind processing a negative outcome so long as it is followed by a positive gain.

Perhaps that common desire to hear the bad news before the good news is why it is common to hear a preacher say, 'I have to tell you about the bad news about sin before I can tell you the good news about Jesus.' The problem with that Gospel communication strategy is that it isn't faithful to the teaching of the Bible on the actual content of the Gospel. Sin certainly precedes Savior in the presentation order of the message, but *both* are key parts of the Gospel. Sin is not a preface; it's a vital chapter. It's not just in the body of the story. It's a key part of the second headline of the news. Consider, for an example, Romans 2:16, where the Apostle Paul wrote:

'On that day when, <u>according to my gospel</u>, God judges the secrets of men by Christ Jesus.'

According to the Apostle Paul, the declaration of the Gospel includes judgment upon men's secrets. The phrase 'men's secrets' is simply an idiom that means the sins of people. The Bible clearly teaches right here in this verse that sin is not a precursor to the Gospel. You don't tell someone the bad news so that they can hear the good news. You tell them the good news which includes important information about sin. There is good news about sin.

How is talking about sin in any way good news? Think of it in these terms. The second headline of the Gospel is **Jesus is putting the world right regarding sin**. More specifically, he is going to right every wrong done to you and by you; he is dealing with personal sin. He is also going to right all that is wrong within you; he is dealing with your indwelling sin. And he is even going to right all that is wrong with creation; he will deal with original sin and all its effects.

The Gospel begins with the simple announcement – Jesus is the Lord. It continues with the straightforward message that this Lord is righting all that is wrong with the world. God is resolved to bring about justice, purity, and glory, and, in Jesus, he is acting in human history for that purpose.

As we did with the first point of the Gospel, let's explore a bit of the depths of this second point, not so that we lose sight of its simplicity, but so that we can increase our understanding of it as well as revel in the good news that there is good news about sin. First, Jesus is going to right every wrong done to you and by you. There will be justice.

Justice

On Monday, February 13, 2017, Libby German and Abby Williams, two teenage girls, went hiking on the Delphi Historic Trail in Delphi, Indiana, a very common activity for the kids in that community. When they did not show up to be picked up a couple hours later, informal, and then formal search parties were organized. Just past midnight, their two bodies were found in the woods.

Those two little girls were wronged. Their parents and grandparents and families and friends were wronged. Lives were taken. Now, they are lost. And that loss will never leave those people in this lifetime. Someone did them wrong.

We all have had an experience of being done wrong, probably not to the extent of those two families, but each one of us has been harmed in some way:

- A child bullied you when you were young. That harassment and intimidation created fear about just going to school. That was wrong.

- A teenager talked viciously behind your back in high school. You were the victim of false accusations and gossip. That was wrong.

- A man took advantage of you. That was wrong.

- A colleague in business shortchanged you. The company cheated you out of what you deserved. That was wrong.

- A loved one betrayed you. You were harmed by someone who was supposed to protect you. That was wrong.

- A group of people rejected you. They treated you differently because of the color of your skin. That was wrong.

The list of the wrong done to us is long and diverse. No one is immune and everyone has felt the sting. It is a seemingly endless catalog of bad news.

So then, isn't it good news that Jesus Christ is going to set it all right? Ponder that reckoning for a moment. The group that rejected you, the loved one who betrayed you, the business that cheated you, the man who took advantage of you, the teenager who spread lies about you, the child who bullied you, the man who murdered those two little girls … nobody is going to get away with any of that. Jesus will right those wrongs. As the Apostle Paul preached:

'God has fixed a day on which he will judge the world in righteousness.' Acts 17:31

Judgment day is coming, and the person appointed to sit on the judgment seat is the Christ. Therefore, you can be assured that all the wrongs against you will be dealt with, every single one. That is such good news!

And listen, all *you* have ever done wrong will be made right as well. This is good news too. After all, don't we all live with some regret related to the pain that our sin has caused others? When our son Matt got in trouble when he was young, he would frequently respond by saying, 'Dad and Mom, can we start over?' It was his cute way of repenting. He wanted to erase what happened that went wrong. He longed for a do over so that he could get it right.

We can all relate to that experience, can't we? You wish it wouldn't have happened, but it did. You would love to turn back time and take it back, but you can't. It is very difficult for you to accept what you did wrong. You cringe inside when it comes to mind, but you have no choice to accept it because it is in the past. No matter what you say or do now, you cannot undo it.

You yearn for resolution, not just related to what others have done wrong to you, but also to quell the soul angst related to the wrong you have done to others. So, rejoice in the Gospel. Jesus is going to put it all right. He is dealing with everyone's personal sin in every way.

If you aren't clear about what personal sin is, it is defined in the Bible as an offense against the righteousness of God. It is a failure to conform to his moral law in the realm of thoughts, desires, words, or deeds. For example, theft is a sinful deed. Gossip is a collection of sinful words. Covetousness is a sinful desire. Thoughts can be sinful as well.

These failures to conform to the moral law of God can be by *commission* – an action that has been done – or by *omission* – something one does *not* do that one *should* do. Consider James 4:17: 'So whoever knows the right thing to do and fails to do it, for him it is sin.' People can sin by what they do and sin by what they do not do.

Contemplate this staggering truth. Every immoral thought, desire, word, and deed from every human being who has ever lived will be adjudicated. Every moral thought, desire, word, and deed that should have been thought, desired, spoken or done, but wasn't, by every human being who has ever lived, will be brought to account. Jesus is going to right every wrong done to you and by you. There will be justice. That's the first part of the Gospel of Jesus as it relates to sin.

The second way sin is included in the good news is: Jesus is going to right all that is wrong within you. There will be justice and there will also be purity.

Purity

Most of my life, I lived about twenty-five miles from downtown Chicago, Illinois. It is not uncommon for people in the suburbs to complain about the violence in the city, particularly on the South Side. Certainly, that complaint is not without warrant. After all, in 2020, 4,033 people were shot resulting in 769 homicides. That's a shocking number. To put it in even more specific perspective, it means that, on average, someone was shot every two hours resulting in two people being killed every single day. Tragic.

The heartbreaking reality of that violence creates both complaint and compassion in suburbanites, but it also leads to a temptation to think wrongly about sin. People in safe middle-class neighborhoods are tempted to think that the fundamental problem with the world isn't in their safe middle-class neighborhoods, but rather in the city or down on the South Side. In other words, they think of sin in *geographic* terms, rather than as a universal *biographic* reality.

The truth is that human nature itself is at the center of what's wrong with the world. Whenever you see a human being, any human being, in some measure, you are looking directly at our problem. There is something wrong, not only out there on the South Side of Chicago or not just with us sometimes when we are having a really bad day in the suburbs or not simply inside the worst people in the world, but *within* all of us at all times. Sin isn't merely personal. It is indwelling.

We have all had experiences when we realized this was true:

- For example, you are going about your normal routine on a typical day when all of a sudden an immoral thought just pops into your head. You don't want it there. You want it to leave. Yet, there it is. How did it just jump into your brain without your permission? Where did it originate?

- Or how about when a corrupt desire suddenly bursts through your soul. You really want to do something wrong, but at the same time you don't. You find yourself having internal conflict.

- Or, remember a time when you used insensitive words and later wondered, 'Where did that outburst come from? Why did I say that in that way? The situation didn't call for that.' You were almost unconsciously harsh.

- Or, have you found yourself doing something you told yourself you would stop doing or at least do much less frequently? We all know what that downward spiral feels like.

- How about when you wake up in a funk and can't shake it all day long? You have a bad attitude and you don't know where it came from and you don't know why it's there and you don't know when it will leave.

The Bible teaches that all these human experiences point to the reality of indwelling sin affecting our mind, dividing our heart, and influencing our will to respond to situations in ways we later regret. In the Scriptures, sin is not merely our personal moral failures. It isn't simply to miss the mark of good behavior. Sin is also a *power* at work in our very nature. Everyone sins, but more importantly, everyone is a sinner.

Isn't it good news, then, that Jesus Christ is going to right all that is wrong within you? That promise of the Gospel is well articulated in 1 John 3:2:

'Beloved, we are God's children now, and what we will be has not yet appeared; but we know that when he appears <u>we shall be like him</u>, because we shall see him as he is.'

That phrase 'we shall be like him' is a reference to Christians becoming like Jesus. We won't become the infinite, eternal, and perfect second person of the Trinity, nor will we become a Jewish man in his thirties. The context of this verse is about purity from sin. Here's what it means.

In Christ, there is no sin. He is pure. In us, there is sin now. We are not pure. When we see him upon our death or his return, we will become like him; that is, we will become pure. In us, there will no longer be any sin.

How incredible is that! Celebrate that reality because it means that on that day:

- The pollution in your mind will be gone. You will only be able to think about what is true, honorable, just, pure, lovely, excellent, and praiseworthy.

- The sickness of your heart will be 100 percent cured. You will only want love, joy, peace, goodness, kindness, gentleness, and faithfulness.

- The struggle with your will is going to end. You will only want the virtue of Christ and you will always do what you want to do. You will never again do something you regret.

The promise of the Gospel is that you are not going to live forever in your current corrupted state. One day, Almighty God will transform you with enduring effect. You will be you, but a metamorphosis will take place. There will be continuity of your personhood, but everlasting discontinuity of your nature. You will become like Jesus. He will make you pure as he is pure. Your mind, heart, and will – your entire inner self – will be made right. He is dealing with your indwelling sin. That's the second part of the Gospel of Jesus as it relates to sin.

Lastly, there will be glory. Jesus is not only going to right what is wrong with humans. He is putting the entire universe right.

Glory

A while back, I went to breakfast with a friend. Upon entering the restaurant, he held the door for a caregiver in charge of an older couple. The husband was blind, and the wife had dementia and struggled severely to walk. And so, the caregiver walked them to breakfast, lunch, and dinner each day from their apartment, one on each arm. They hobbled slowly and painfully, afflicted, and struggling ... sadly, it was not hard to see death looming over them. As I watched them walk away when they were done, I thought, 'I hate sin. And I love Jesus Christ.' That might seem like an odd response to you, but it comes from a Biblical understanding of sin.

Now, to be crystal clear, I am NOT at all suggesting that the elderly couple's specific maladies were caused by their specific moral failures. I don't think his blindness was caused by his character defects. Likewise, I don't connect her dementia to a pattern of rebellion earlier in her life. I am not advocating for the idea of a tit-for-tat view of immorality and physical suffering as if there is always a direct line from personal sin to bodily ailments. That is not what the Bible means by original sin.

Rather, the Scriptures teach that original sin is the *root* of all that is wrong with the world. That is, the initial rebellion of humanity against God has damaged the entire universe resulting in all the problems that plague us. The Apostle Paul stated this bondage to corruption most clearly in his Epistle to the Roman Church:

'The creation was subjected to futility.' Romans 8:20

We all know the world is not right. A tornado rips through a nearby town. Almost every extended family holiday has some sort of argument. A friend is diagnosed with Multiple Sclerosis. As soon as you get your life and house organized, someone messes it up. A person close to you dies. All of a sudden you cannot see words on a page clearly when it is close to you. Your hairline is receding, and your muscles are drooping, and belly is growing, and your car is breaking down.

The Bible's explanation for all those experiences is original sin. The first people sinned. That sin wasn't just harmful to their relationship with God. It was catastrophic for the entire created order. It unleashed the power and the presence of sin into the world causing disease, disability, discord, decay, disorder, disaster and even death.

Sin is personal. It is moral failure. Sin is also indwelling. It is the power at work in our nature causing moral failure. But, it is also original. It is a presence that has shackled the right functioning of the world.

I find that most people struggle with this aspect of sin, finding it hard to believe or difficult to understand. Strangely enough, I think there is help for us in middle school chemistry combined with some home economics. The difference between a chemical change and a physical change provides a clarifying illustration for this topic.

A physical change is change that can be undone. Consider a tossed salad. You take lettuce and whatever other ingredients you like out of the refrigerator and the pantry. You grab a large bowl and those big wooden utensils. You set them all out on your kitchen counter and you mix them together. The result is a tossed salad. A tossed salad is a physical change because it can be undone by human beings. In other words, you can un-toss it, separating the croutons from the carrots from the lettuce from the bacon, etc. You can even wash off the salad dressing! It can be undone.

On the contrary, a chemical change is a change that cannot be undone. Consider the act of baking a cake. You do the same as you did with tossed salad. You get all the ingredients you need: flour, sugar, eggs, chocolate, etc. You mix them together, put them in the cake pan, and slide it into the oven for baking. Several minutes later, it comes out as a cake. Unlike a tossed salad, a baked cake is a chemical change, not a physical one. You cannot undo it. You can't un-bake it and un-mix it.

If I came over for dessert and asked you to get the eggs out of the cake because I'd prefer to eat them instead, you would look at me sideways and say, 'That's impossible!' And you would be right.

Think of original sin like a chemical change, not a physical one. Sin is a defiling presence that has mixed itself inseparably into the human being such that human beings cannot separate themselves from sin. We cannot undo it. Furthermore, through us, sin has been unleashed into the world such that its presence has fundamentally changed the world. The cake has been baked and it is impossible for us to un-bake it.

But, the good news is that Jesus Christ is going do that which seems impossible. He has promised to undo all the effects of original sin. Isn't that incredible? Think about it. That means cancer, confusion, rusty and crumbling bridges, stillborn babies, town-engulfing earthquakes, ethnic tension, cerebral palsy are not going to be forever experiences. All of that and more will be permanently eliminated from God's world. The universe is in bondage to corruption now, but one day it will be set free and transformed. Glory is coming. That's the third part of the Gospel of Jesus Christ as it relates to sin.

Therefore, the next time you think of sin as the bad news that must precede the good news, remember that the Bible teaches that sin is part of the Gospel of Jesus. Namely, Jesus is putting the world right regarding sin. That is always good news.

And, at this halfway point of this explanation of the Gospel, keep it clear in your mind. The message inescapably revolves around Jesus of Nazareth. It is about him. That message starts with the announcement that Jesus is the Lord. He is the flawless, God-man with all authority in Heaven and on Earth. That's the first headline.

The message continues with the declaration that he is righting all that is wrong with this world. He is displeased with how humans have behaved, what humans have become and even how the universe is functioning as a result. Since he is the Lord, he is acting on that displeasure to bring about the justice, purity, and glory he wants. That's the second headline of the message.

Now, as we approach the third headline of the Gospel, it is important to pause and address what could be the elephant in the room in your mind. Perhaps you have had a lingering and growing thought in the back of your mind while reading this chapter that this good news about sin isn't really good news because you are a sinner with whom Jesus is displeased.

In other words, if the Christ is going to judge the world for sin, how in the world will I escape the consequences of that judgment since I have sinned? If the King is going to destroy the power of sin, how will I not be destroyed since that power is at work in my heart? If the Son is going to eliminate the presence of sin, how will I not be eliminated since sin is 'baked into' my very being? If we are at the center of what is wrong with the world, won't we have a serious problem as Jesus puts it all right? This book is entitled *Always Good News*, but halfway through the headlines, it seems like it isn't necessarily good news for everyone. Perhaps you are thinking that it is not good for you at all.

Well, if you have this concern, the second half of the Gospel will alleviate it. It begins with the announcement that Jesus is the only Savior of sinners. Then, it explains how he saves people just like you through his judging, purifying, and glorifying work.

4

Jesus is the Only Savior of Sinners

✳   ✳   ✳

AS a professional basketball fan in the 1990s, I watched every Chicago Bulls game I could possibly watch. There was simply nothing better in those days than tuning in to Michael Jordan doing his thing. He was one-of-a-kind; a unique combination of athleticism, talent, work ethic and will to win.

So, like virtually everyone else who followed him, I was stunned and disappointed when Michael retired at thirty years old, after winning three straight championships, to become a minor-league baseball player. I continued to watch the Bulls the following year, but I knew that there was no chance of a four-peat. Without Jordan, their reign was over because no one could do what he could do. He was the only one capable of leading that franchise to an NBA title.

Now, those are words of affirmation about Michael's excellence, right? They aren't meant to diminish others. They are simply true and proved to be so when the Bulls didn't win the title for two years during his retirement, but then won it three straight years again after he left baseball to return to hoops full time. No Bulls team could win a championship except through Jordan. He was the one who enabled Chicago fans to celebrate a basketball dynasty. That's a fact of history and those words are intended to rejoice in what only Michael could do.

Yet, for some reason, when similar words are spoken about Jesus, they are often viewed, not as positive about his greatness, but as negative about his exclusivity. After the Apostle Peter was arrested by the Sanhedrin for preaching the Gospel, he reiterated the message's third point to them by saying,

'And there is salvation in no one else, for there is no other name under heaven given among men by which we must be saved.' Acts 4:12

Those words from Peter are like what many fans said in the 1990s about Michael Jordan. They aren't intended to put others down, but rather to focus on the one-of-a-kind greatness of Christ, his unique combination of authority, virtue, and divinity. According to Peter, it is an obvious fact of history that no one else has beaten sin and death like Jesus did. He's the champ.

Obviously then, to him, there is salvation in no one else other than Jesus. He is the only one fit to put the world right regarding sin and the only one able to save sinners while he puts it right. Further, that reality is obviously worth celebrating as good news because we are all on the same human team dealing with the same human condition.

Looking back in history now, we can see that it was a mistake, then, for the religious leaders of Peter's day to be greatly disturbed by this message, as if Jesus was preventing them from doing something that they were completely capable of doing on their own.

The reality is they had no means by which they could truly and totally make amends with God for all that they had done wrong.

Likewise, they couldn't overcome all that was wrong within them, nor could they fix all that is wrong with the world. No sinner has the means to do any of those things.

When Jesus himself said, 'No one comes to the Father except through me,' he meant that all religions and forms of spirituality without him are like all Bulls teams without Jordan. They simply cannot win against the foe they are facing. It is a hopeless situation. That's the point that the Bible is making.

Without Jesus, no one can escape the penalty of sin, no one can overcome the power of sin, and no one can get rid of the presence of sin. We cannot save ourselves from sin and nobody can save us except for the Lord. That's why this news about him is so good.

Jesus is the only Savior of sinners. Only the Christ can pay for our personal sin. Only the King can defeat our indwelling sin. Only the Son of God can undo the effects of original sin. That's the third headline of the Gospel. He provides hope to the hopeless.

As we have done in the past two chapters, without losing sight of the main point here, let's explore his hope-infusing work in those three aspects to understand why the Lord alone is qualified to save sinners and why it is such good news. First, the death of Jesus is the only means capable of saving us from God's judgment on our personal sin. There is some deep theological stuff here. Put your thinking cap on.

The Death of Jesus

When I was young, I took something that didn't belong to me and developed this intense feeling of guilt about it. Perhaps you have had a similar experience. You did something you knew you weren't supposed to do, and you feel bad inside. You are ashamed. We all live with standards. When we break them, we have regrets. And when we think of guilt, we most often think of a personal, subjective feeling like that.

There is another kind of guilt, though. It is the forensic type. It occurs when you break the law. One day, I paused in my car at the entrance of Wal-Mart to pick up one of my sons. I was there for less than a minute as he hopped into the back seat. A few weeks later, I received a ticket in the mail indicating that I was parked illegally in a no parking zone. Apparently, a police officer was nearby taking pictures of the license plates of anyone who stopped in front of the store.

Incredulous, I went before the judge to plead my case. I couldn't believe law enforcement didn't have anything better to do with their time than issue violations like that. Yet, the reality is, even though I didn't feel guilty in the slightest bit, I did, in fact, break the law. That was made very clear to me that day. I was *pronounced* guilty and had to pay the fine as punishment. People who break laws should be punished commensurate with the laws they break. It is called justice.

Thus it is with humanity and God. Everyone has broken God's law to some degree, and we will all stand before Jesus Christ to give an account for our lives. You will appear before the Judge of the universe to have the case of your life adjudicated.

Now, as you envision that heavenly court date, you may not actually feel a sense of guilt about your life in the aggregate. In other words, sure, you have messed up some, but overall, you view yourself as a relatively good person. You may have a sense of skepticism that your 'lesser' sins are a problem with God, like it is simply misbehavior that's not worth policing. Furthermore, the idea that your misdeeds warrant a penalty could even be offensive to you. Perhaps you have some inclination to plead your case with him.

While that may be a common viewpoint, it is not a helpful one because the judgment will not compare you with the rest of humanity, or compare you with your own view of what should be judged. The judgment will be your entire sinful life contrasted with all the holiness of your Creator. When that assessment happens, the Bible indicates we will all be pronounced guilty for our personal sin and sentenced accordingly. There will be justice.

The good news about that justice is that God can show mercy to you through the death of Jesus. If you were feeling uncomfortable in the last chapter reading about Jesus judging the world, wondering how you would escape the consequences of that judgment since you are keenly aware of your sin, read this section with particular focus and rejoice in it.

How does the demise of a man who lived a couple thousand years ago help you with your looming death and impending judgment? Though it may seem like distant, unrelated history, *his* death is the most pertinent event of *your* future. Here's why.

Since God is just, he must punish your sin. He isn't willing to overlook it. He is not going to give you a wink and a nod in the heavenly courtroom, and announce, 'Joe is not really that guilty. It's no big deal. I'll let it slide.' God will not do that because that's called corruption, and he does not have an ounce of corruption in his nature. The demands of justice regarding your sin must be satisfied.

And if you think about it, you really don't want God to behave in a dishonest manner, do you? Do you want him to act fraudulently with people who have sinned against you? Should he release and reward them? How about the worst evildoers you can think of? Would it be okay to let them off the hook too? Of course not. We all want a just God, not a corrupt one.

Well, the Gospel announces the good news that Jesus satisfied those demands so that you, and anyone else, can experience mercy. On that Roman cross, Jesus of Nazareth offered his sinless life to God as payment for your sin. He experienced every dimension of Hell on your behalf, suffering all the wrath of God for all your transgressions. He died in your place.

Since he is the Christ, the perfect person, he is the only one who could lay down his life for us in this way. He is the only acceptable sacrifice. No one else's life qualifies for this exchange because everyone else has sinned in some way. And since he is God the Son, he is also the only one who could bear infinite wrath. No one else can endure the fury of God's judgment on the sins of humanity because everyone else is a finite being. As the Apostle John wrote:

> **'He is the propitiation for our sins, and not for ours only but also for the sins of the whole world.' 1 John 2:2**

Moreover, through his atoning death, he has secured the capacity to expiate forensic guilt. In other words, he made amends with God for us and has, therefore, achieved the right to release us. When you stand before God in judgment, Jesus can justify you. If *you* plead *your* case, you will be doomed, but *he* can plead *his* case on your behalf. Without compromising God's justice in any way, he can extend mercy.

Do you see now why the death of Jesus is the only means capable of saving us from God's judgment on our personal sin? It is the only hope we have for a pardon. That's why we celebrate him. He is the only Savior of sinners. Similarly, his resurrection life is the only means capable of saving sinners from the power of indwelling sin. This is really good news too.

The Resurrection of Jesus

There is a tale in the Christian community of Pierre Paul Roux, a colleague of Louis Pasteur who lived during the late 19th and early 20th centuries. His granddaughter died of black diphtheria, so he was determined to save others from it. He theorized that if a creature was infected by the bacteria, fought it off and lived, its blood could be used to cure the infected who were dying. The victorious one could bring that victory to others.

According to some oral tradition about his life, he gathered twenty horses and swabbed them on their faces with the diphtheria bacteria. Every horse developed the symptoms of the infection, fell to the ground, and died, except for one. It lingered on its side for several days, but then, miraculously recovered and stood upright. The horse won the battle against the power of the infection and was raised to live again.

Supposedly, he and other scientists drew as much of its blood as possible and immediately rushed to a nearby municipal hospital in Paris where they pushed their way past the staff into a ward where babies were quarantined. With the blood of that victorious horse, they inoculated every one of them, redeeming hundreds of lives. Those children were saved by the blood of an overcomer.

That tale has a Christian parallel of good news about the resurrection of Jesus. Since the beginning of humanity, people have been infected with sin. At the most profound level, it is what is ruling us, and it is what is killing us. But like Pierre Paul Roux, God has seen our plight and is determined to save us from this insidious spiritual disease.

To do that, the Son of God incarnated to live a natural human life under God's law without breaking any of it; Jesus fulfilled the law with his sinless life. Then, like the horse in that tale, he laid down his innocent life and miraculously picked it up again.

Jesus knew no sin, but he *became sin* on behalf of sinners so that by his death and resurrection he would not only pay the penalty for sin, but also personally defeat the power of sin.

Having achieved victory over sin in life by fighting off every temptation, he then conquered sin's greatest consequence – death itself. Thus, now the Victorious One can share his victory with others. As a result of his shed blood, the one and only Overcomer can empower people to overcome their own indwelling sin. Such good news! There will be justice and there will be purity.

Obviously, he doesn't purify us from sin by an injection of his actual blood into our bodies through a needle as Pierre Paul Roux did. These are spiritual realities, not physical, so the way he does it is spiritual. Having ascended to his heavenly throne, he can now pour his Holy Spirit into your heart, and thus, dethrone sin in you. That's the way he does it.

That act doesn't completely and immediately eliminate all the sin within you, but it does break the power of its dominion over your life and replace it with the very presence of God. The Lord reigns over all and he applies that reign to people by sending his Spirit to reign in the throne room of their souls. It's quite a genius strategy. Since the human problem is within, King Jesus conquers us from within. The Apostle John put it this way ...

> 'No one born of God makes a practice of sinning, for God's seed abides in him; and he cannot keep on sinning, because he has been born of God.' 1 John 3:9

Christians are people who have been born of God. That born again experience was the result of the Lord putting the compelling purity of the Holy Spirit, his seed, within us. Though the presence of sin remains in the Christian's life, the Spirit leads us out of our habitual *practice* of sin. That is how he is saving us from our indwelling sin. It is an internal purification by the power of his resurrection life. We used to be slaves to sin, but we have been set free from that cruel oppressor to serve our kind and gentle master Jesus.

And I invite you to consider ... who else can do that work?

- Can religions? Which of their founders have beaten sin and death in this way?

- Can human counselors or improvement programs? What can they do but offer advice and modify outward behavior patterns? That's a helpful work, but can they change the human heart?

- What about education? Can instruction do the work of saving? Why would more information lead to inner ontological transformation?

- Can government? How can legislative authority help when what we need is spiritual power?

- How about your spouse or your best friend? Can they save you? Well, aren't they sinners who need saving too? How will they rescue you?

- Can you do it on your own? How can you possibly alter the composition of your own soul?

When you consider all the other options, it is not hard to realize the truth. Only Jesus can save us from the power of our indwelling sin. He is the only Savior of sinners. Lastly on this third part of the good news, Jesus' return is the only means capable of saving sinners from original sin.

The Return of Jesus

In 2000, our son Matt was born with postaxial hypoplasia in his left leg. This condition can have a variety of bone abnormalities. In his case, his left femur, tibia, and fibula were not the same length as those on his right and would likely never 'catch up' during his growth to maturity. In addition, of the twenty-six bones that most people have in their left foot, Matt had just two. The doctor was unable to determine if those two were phalanges or metatarsals as there were no other bones whatsoever inside the flesh that bore a vague resemblance to a typical human foot.

The painful solution to this condition was amputation of that foot when he was just seven months old to create a heel pad on the distal end of his limb. That surgery allowed him to be fitted for a prosthetic left leg which could address both disabilities created by the condition. First, it provided a substitute foot so that he would be able to walk. Second, the knee down nature of the device created a way to artificially lengthen the left leg as he grew so that it could always be the same length as the right leg.

Now, as his parents, my wife and I have obviously done all we can to help Matt with his disability. That's what you do when you face something wrong in life, particularly with those people you love most. You do your best to make it right. Further, we have celebrated the advancements of technology that have helped him. Isn't it amazing that he was the first of our four children to walk? I'll never forget when he stood up and ambled across our kitchen floor at just 11 months old. Such a precious memory.

Matt even played baseball in high school. I can still vividly envision the homerun he hit into the parking lot at Wheeling or the double off the wall with the bases loaded to beat an undefeated Buffalo Grove team. We rejoice in all that he has been able to do physically as well as in all that people have done to help him overcome the challenges presented by his body.

Yet, we also clearly understand what cannot be done for him. We cannot give him a new left leg and foot with all the bones and proper development. Oh, how we wish we could! We would give up our own bones in a heartbeat so that he could have them. But, alas, we can't make the situation right in that way.

You see, none of the good that has been done removes the sense of loss we feel for him regarding what cannot be done. In other words, we have hopes for his earthly life that can and are being realized, and for that we are very grateful. But we have no hope for true physical wholeness for him on this planet. That isn't available to him, or to anyone for that matter, in this life. It awaits the next.

The world is not right and there are some things we can't resolve:

- Hurricanes tear through the Gulf of Mexico and flood multiple states. We know they are coming. We prepare for them, but we can't stop them.

- We create laws to stop racism and protest when it happens, but it still lingers in the hearts of people.

- We organize our house and care for our lawn, but the laundry piles up and drought and grubs turn the grass brown.

- We bombard cancer with chemotherapy and radiation, but it returns to grow until it overtakes life.

- We try to keep the winter salt off the car but rust invariably develops causing a breakdown.

Humanity continues to strive for utopia, but original sin makes it impossible to achieve. Remember the illustration of a chemical change in Chapter 4. The cake has been baked and no one can do anything about it; no one, that is, except Jesus.

The good news about the Lord is that he has promised to return to Earth to right all that is wrong with this world. He is not just interested in justice and purity. He is determined to usher in glory. The Apostle John saw a vision of the Lord doing just that and recorded it in Revelation 21. About this promise, Jesus said:

'Behold, I am making all things new. Write this down for these words are trustworthy and true.' Revelation 21:5

Jesus is going to make *everything* new. Forty days after his resurrection, he ascended into Heaven. At an unknown time in the future, he will descend from Heaven in the same form and in the same way that he left. After he returns, he will continue his work of making everything new by giving Christians new bodies, patterned after his resurrection body.

Whereas our current bodies are flawed, weak, natural, sinful, and perishable, our new bodies will be like his – complete, invulnerable, spiritual, holy, and immortal. With the same power he used to raise himself from the dead, he will raise you, Christian. He's not going to enter your grave and perform CPR to reanimate your old body. He's going to transform your current one, whether it is alive or dead when he returns, into a glorified one.

Then, with the same power Jesus used to create the cosmos, he is going to create a new glorified world. Since the Scripture is silent on the scope of the change, we don't know if he plans to resurrect the entire universe, just the Milky Way, or simply our solar system. It is difficult to have certainty on how pervasive sin is and how thoroughly it has corrupted what God has made.

What we do know is that the world that we currently experience will be transformed such that all the effects of original sin will be overcome. Jesus will eliminate the presence of sin, setting the creation itself free from its bondage to corruption. And the results will be astounding.

Disease will end and everlasting health will begin. Disabilities will be made permanently whole. Discord will give way to constant harmony. Decay will reverse into perpetual growth. Tranquility will replace disorder and success will supplant disaster. Even death itself will die. Revelation 21:4 describes his return in this way:

> **'He will wipe away every tear from their eyes, and death shall be no more, neither shall there be mourning, nor crying, nor pain anymore, for the former things have passed away.'**

This is the Gospel hope we have for our son Matt, ourselves, and everyone else: a New Heaven and a New Earth where righteousness dwells. Only Jesus, the Son of God, can create this eternal life. He is the only one who can save us from all that is currently wrong, the only Savior of sinners.

Hopefully, this Gospel is coming into crystal clear focus for you as well as giving you great joy. We are now 75 percent of the way through it. The depth of the message can be somewhat disorienting, but the simplicity is evident. The headlines are clear. First, Jesus is the LORD. Second, he is putting the world right regarding SIN. Third, he is the only SAVIOR of sinners. And, fourth, now that you know he alone can save you through his judging, purifying and glorifying work, the Gospel concludes with how he does that. Jesus saves sinners by grace through FAITH. Don't miss this last part. It is always good news too.

5

Jesus is Saving Sinners by
Grace through Faith

* * *

WHEN the devout Christian and famous scientist, Sir Michael Faraday was dying in 1867, some journalists questioned him as to his scientific speculations for a life after death. His response was bold and unequivocal. 'Speculations!' he said, 'I know nothing about speculations. I'm resting on certainties. I know that my redeemer lives and because he lives, I shall live also.'

What a great way to sum up the last point of the good news about Jesus. Sir Faraday had faith in Jesus. That is, he looked backward in history in faith at the Cross, and relied on the work of his Redeemer, the Christ, as the only way to get right and stay right with God. He believed Jesus paid the penalty for his personal sin.

He also looked upward in faith to the throne of the universe, relying on King Jesus for the power to defeat sin. He believed the Redeemer not only accomplished the work of atonement in the past, but also _lives_ right now for the good of his redeemed people today, to empower them to fight their indwelling sin. The tomb is empty. Jesus reigns. Therefore, I can change to become more like him. That's faith too.

Furthermore, Sir Faraday looked forward in faith to the day beyond his death, relying on the Son of God to resurrect him.

Because Jesus lives, he believed he would live too, like him and with him in a new glorified world. That faith helped him cope with the effects of original sin, most prominently death. These are all expressions of faith: backward-looking reliance, upward-looking reliance, and forward-looking reliance.

To be clear, I am not arguing for three separate types of faith, like you can have one but not the other. When you have any faith at all, you have some degree of all three because all three are aspects of your one faith. What I am suggesting then, is that thinking about faith in terms of these three aspects will increase your understanding of faith, its place in the Gospel, and why it's always good news.

Furthermore, be sure to keep it clear in your mind that this three-fold faith is a gift of God's grace. It is not something that a person creates on their own, independent from the activity of the Lord. That perspective is key to seeing this fourth point of the Gospel as good news. It is also what the Apostle Paul taught in Ephesians 2:8-9:

> 'For by grace you have been saved through faith. And this is not your own doing; it is the gift of God, not a result of works, so that no one may boast.'

The fourth headline of the Gospel is **Jesus is saving sinners by grace through faith.** Isn't that good news!? If you have any inclination to trust in Jesus to be saved from personal, indwelling, and original sin, any proclivity in you whatsoever, that is a sign that God is at work in you to save you. No matter how small or how weak your reliance is, if you are relying on the person, work and promises of Jesus of Nazareth, that means God has given you this gift of faith.

So, don't get down when you struggle with doubt, even when your soul feels like a combat zone between doubt and faith. Doubt is not a sign of unbelief. Doubt is actually an indication of the presence of at least some faith. And faith can only be present because God has given it. It's the gift of God.

Be encouraged by the presence of any amount of faith in you at all. It is the miraculous work of the Lord. Let's gain some insight to this final headline of the good news starting with the backward-looking aspect of faith in Jesus.

Looking Back

At the end of 2019, our son John graduated from Indiana Wesleyan University with a double major in Finance and Economics. He began his job search in January of 2020 looking for work in the financial services industry. John is a bright guy who is good with numbers. He also has a compassionate heart and loves to help people. Those strengths make financial planning a great vocation for him.

Now, job searches almost always involve a résumé. If you want a job, you must have a document that shows why the company would want to hire you. It lists all your qualifications, like education, experience, and references. John was enthused to show me his résumé for my fatherly input, but my advice to him was that the most important factor in landing a job is not the content of a résumé. It is the quality of your relationships. Getting work is often about who you know and who knows you.

Well, the Apostle Paul had a similar thought for the first-century church in Philippi. They were wrestling with the importance of a spiritual résumé to be in a right relationship with God. I am sure you have wrestled with the same issue. How good is good enough to be qualified for Heaven? That was their question.

And Paul's word to them was like my word to John, but even stronger in force. He told them that salvation from sin is most definitely not earned by your spiritual résumé because he had the best one ever and it didn't get him right with God.

Since you may not be familiar with Paul's spiritual résumé, let me tell you a bit about it. It started with the best spiritual education. Paul grew up as a young boy memorizing the entire Hebrew Bible, learning what it all meant and practicing how it applied to life. As a young man, he studied under the greatest Torah teacher of his time, Gamaliel. As an adult, he was accepted to the most elite orthodox Jewish scholarly orders, the Pharisees.

Paul also had the best spiritual experience. He knew all the laws of God and was totally committed to following them. He came out of the womb obeying and perfectly kept the behaviors that were mandated by the Old Testament. He never violated Torah. In fact, he kept hundreds of other commands that were not even in the Bible but were based on its principles. He was blameless in terms of the legalistic righteousness as defined in his time.

And Paul had the best spiritual references: Abraham, Moses, Isaac, Jacob, and Benjamin. You see, he wasn't a regular Israelite. The very blood of the fathers of God's covenants flowed through him. He was religious royalty with a flawless pedigree; a purebred, as Hebrew as it gets.

If anyone had reason to be confident in their own spiritual resume, it was the Apostle Paul. And, before he met Jesus, he did consider it profit. He thought his education, experiences and references were more than capable to justify him before God. He believed that his good deeds paid for his personal sin. Moreover, he even seemed to believe that he had some righteousness left over.

But on the road to Damascus, he found out from the risen Christ himself that his spiritual résumé was worse than worthless. He learned the spiritual parallel of the vocational lesson I shared with my son John. It's about who you know and who knows you. In this case, it is about Jesus. Look at what Paul wrote:

> **'and be found in him, not having a righteousness of my own that comes from the law, but that which comes through faith in Christ, the righteousness from God that depends on faith.'**
> **Philippians 3:9**

The Bible teaches that true righteousness before God comes, not from us to God by our works as listed on a spiritual résumé in the present. No way. Our good deeds cannot atone for our misdeeds. Rather, true righteousness before God comes *from God to us* through our faith in Jesus' perfect fulfillment of the law and substitutionary work of atonement on the Cross in the past.

Jesus saves sinners from the eternal consequences of their personal sin by grace through backward-looking faith. He shows mercy to us because we rely on the faithfulness of his earthly life in the first century, not our own résumé of righteousness in the twenty-first century.

If your mind is thinking in these ways and your heart is warm to these thoughts, that is a sign that God is at work in you. He's creating and growing faith in your soul. Isn't that good news? The peace and joy of it is quite overwhelming.

It means that you can be assured right now that you will escape the consequences of your sin when Christ returns to judge the world. God has no wrath for you. As Romans 8:1 promises, 'There is therefore now no condemnation for those who are in Christ Jesus.'

The Lord is going to right every wrong done to you and by you in such a way that he will not condemn you. Instead, he will save you. Your faith now, no matter how small, is a sign of that guaranteed future. You have been declared righteous ahead of the judgment. It is so certain that the Bible describes Christians as 'saved,' in the past tense. Jesus has justified you through your faith. Isn't that amazing and wonderful?

Let that glorious truth sink into your soul. It is the first aspect of faith, backward looking to deal with your personal sin. And it's always good news. Because, though we are no longer in the habit of practicing sin, we still do commit sins. So, it's wonderful to remember every day that God has made a provision for our forgiveness in Jesus Christ, and nothing can stop him from pardoning us, not even our Christian sin. The second aspect of faith worth celebrating is how it is upward looking to battle your indwelling sin.

Looking Up

In the summer of 2019, our only daughter Alyssa got married. I had the wonderful privilege of both walking her down the aisle to give her away to her husband as her father, but also officiating the wedding as a pastor.

Our son-in-law's father is a pastor too. He welcomed our guests and asked me that famous question, 'Who gives this woman to be married to this man?' I got to say, 'Her mother and I,' gave her a big hug, put their hands together and then walked up around them to preach and lead them in the recitation of their vows. It was a very rich and meaningful experience filled with great joy. I love being a dad and I love being her dad.

And occasions like those are cause for reminiscing, aren't they? They are defining moments in life when you then look back on your life together and think about all the special times you had up to that point. I remembered all the bedtime stories, teaching the ABC's, playing dolls, lunch dates, school functions and sports teams. A lot of that stuff comes flooding back into your mind when your daughter is standing right in front of you wearing a wedding dress.

Like the time she took two hours to jump into my arms as a toddler from the side of the pool into the shallow end. She was so cautious. I had to coax her and coax her. Standing in that pool, I remember wanting to reach into her heart and strengthen her faith in my ability to catch her and keep her safe.

She kept looking down at the water and I kept saying, 'Don't look down at the water. Look up at me and trust me. I'm your daddy. Of course, I'm going to catch you.'

Eventually, she jumped. The power of my persistent words and calming presence overcame the doubt of her mind. Now, I think that is a great picture for this Gospel topic of upward reliance on Christ in our battle against indwelling sin.

Like Alyssa staring down at the water, our natural tendency is to keep looking at the challenge of our character flaws and get immobilized by them. It's easy to believe that we just can't change, that we will always struggle with particular bad habits. The depravity of our own souls can be quite overwhelming, especially when we fixate on it.

But the good news is Jesus calls to us as the King of the Universe saying, 'Look up at me and trust me. I am real and I am sovereign. I can save you from the inside out. Believe it!' That is the path to being rescued from the destructive power of sin. The Apostle John wrote in 1 John 5:4 about this dynamic of faith as the operating principle of the Gospel:

'For everyone who has been born of God overcomes the world. And this is the victory that has overcome the world – our faith.'

This is the victory. What is this? Our faith. The Bible teaches that God grants people real spiritual power to fight sin. Faith is the victory by which we access that power to overcome the world, by which we battle and defeat all that is wrong within us. We depend on him.

The good news is that we are not alone in our struggle to change. Jesus is with us, and he is for us. He saves sinners from the power of their indwelling sin by grace through upward-looking faith, relying on his Holy Spirit, not merely our own strength.

You see, the Gospel announces, not just that people *can* change, but that Jesus *is actively changing people* through their faith. He is at work causing people to trust in him by the force of his Word and the strength of his presence.

I experienced this power of the Gospel in that way early in my Christian life. I was an alcoholic and a drug addict. After I put my faith in Christ for the first time, the Lord made it clear to me through the Bible that my substance abuse habits displeased him and were destroying my life. So, in April of 1992, I decided to stop using. The immediate result of that decision was being curled up in the fetal position detoxing from all the substances my body was accustomed to consuming.

For days, weeks, and months following that decision, the cravings resurfaced to varying degrees. Every time I was tempted, I cried out in prayer to Jesus Christ with the faith that I did have so that he would give me more faith to continually beat that specific sin.

In a way, I imitated the man who met Jesus as recorded in Mark 9. He cried out, 'I believe, help my unbelief!' He looked up to Jesus in the faith that he was given to get more faith. That's what I did, and the Lord rescued me from the throes of addiction such that I have been clean and sober for thirty years.

That's not just my experience. It is not simply a sobriety method that worked for me. It is the dynamic of the Gospel that countless numbers of people have experienced throughout all of history enabling them to overcome all manner of sin and temptation.

When a particular obedience is too difficult for the current size of our faith, the King can make us stronger. When we have a desire to change, but that desire isn't strong enough to cause our will to bring about that change, God can intervene.

This dynamic of the Gospel applies to you too. Are you struggling in some way? Do you feel powerless when it comes to indwelling sin? Is that bad habit getting the best of you again? There is good news for you. Christ has everything you need. Get on your knees, look up in faith and call on him for more strength or even more faith.

And when he answers that prayer, enjoy not just the power of overcoming that specific sin, but also the assurance that his work in you now means he is saving you. Be encouraged about the battle within you. It is a sign, not that you are a bad Christian, but that you are indeed a Christian. When I wasn't a Christian, there was no battle inside. The battle is evidence of God's gift of faith to you.

Jesus is saving sinners from the power of our indwelling sin by grace through upward-looking faith. That's the second aspect of faith worth celebrating in the Gospel every day. Third, and lastly, Jesus will save sinners from the effects of original sin by grace through forward-looking faith.

Looking Forward

When Baptist pastor Dr. W. B. Hinson from Portland, OR, became terminally ill, he told his church about what he did in response to the news of his looming death. He said, 'I walked out to where I live five miles of this city, and I looked across at that mountain that I love, and I looked at the river in which I rejoice, and I looked at the stately trees that are always God's own poetry to my soul. Then in the evening I looked up into the great sky where God was lighting his lamps and I said: "I may not see you many more times, but Mountain, I shall be alive when you are gone, and River, I shall be alive when you cease running toward the sea and Stars, I shall be alive when you have fallen from your sockets in the great pulling down of the material universe."'

That's some inspiring faith. You see, faith is not just looking back at the Cross for forgiveness from Jesus Christ. Neither is faith only limited to looking up at the heavenly throne for more power from King Jesus to change our sin habits. Faith also looks forward to the Son of God's return as the main way to cope with this fallen world. That's part of the Gospel. In Pastor Hinson's case, faith was the main way he dealt with the disease that was leading to his death.

Romans 8:23-24 provides a helpful description of this aspect of faith and makes clear it is included in the Gospel message:

> **'And not only the creation, but we ourselves, who have the firstfruits of the Spirit, groan inwardly as we wait eagerly for adoption as sons, the redemption of our bodies. For in this hope we were saved.'**

The Bible says creation is leaning forward with great anticipation. The universe is on the edge of its seat wanting Jesus to return, groaning with eagerness. And so are people of faith. We are on the edge of our seat in life, crying out in our hearts for our new resurrection bodies. That is part of the hope in which we were saved. In other words, forward-looking reliance on Jesus to glorify us and the rest of creation is contained within the Gospel message. That's Romans 8:24.

In 2016, I separated my shoulder. The doctor put some metal pins of some sort in there that basically held it together so that it would heal properly. One week during my rehab, it was hurting. I overdid it at the fitness center, and I was having trouble lifting it when our youngest son Ben said, 'Dad, are those pins going to be in your body forever?' I replied, 'Not forever.' And he said, 'Well, until you get your new body? Will they be in there until then?' I said, 'Yes, and I can't wait for my new body!'

That is the vocabulary of forward-looking faith. Did I go to the doctor for surgery? Yes. Did I go to physical therapy? Sure. Did I use earthly means to manage the situation as best I could? Of course. Did I pray for healing? You bet. But how did I ultimately cope? By faith I said, 'I can't wait for my new body!' and I meant it with all my heart. That was and still is my perspective. Faith is what has helped me cope with all the miseries of this fallen world caused by original sin. And that's part of the Gospel. It's another reason it is always good news.

You see, the good news isn't that we will float around in bodiless souls in an ethereal heaven forever, but that we will walk in new bodies on a renewed Earth with the Lord and everyone else who has relied on him for salvation. We will live forever in a physical *and* spiritual paradise where sin is no more. Thanks be to Jesus for that!

In summary about this last headline of the Gospel, it is good news for Christians in these three ways:

- Jesus has saved us from our personal sin through our backward-looking faith. God has definitively and permanently declared that he is *for us* because of the work of his Christ. We will not be condemned for our sin in this life or the next.

- Jesus is saving us from our indwelling sin through our upward-looking faith. God is actively working *in us* to make us more virtuous like his King. We are not on our own in the battle against sin in this life.

- Jesus will save us from original sin through our forward-looking faith. God will do *to us* exactly what he did to his Son – resurrection. We will overcome this world after we die.

Now, as I wrap up this in-depth explanation of the good news about Jesus of Nazareth, it is good to summarize, not just why it is good news, but also why it is so good every day. Granted, we live in a bad news world. That is a given. We all experience it regularly. Every time something good happens, it seems there is a 'yeah that is good, but ...' moment of bad news that brings us down.

While that is true, do you see now how the good news about Jesus is able to transcend all the bad news and put every bit of it in a hope-filled framework? It doesn't eliminate the negative experiences we are having. It doesn't make it all go away, but do you understand how it is able to genuinely respond to every bit of trouble we get ourselves into and every ounce of tribulation this world throws at us with a 'yeah that is bad, but ...' perspective? Think about it. What bad things are happening in your life?

Did you do something wrong this week? Is your conscience troubled? You sinned and it feels like it is haunting you and hanging over your head. That's not a good experience at all, but the good news is Jesus forgives sinners. The wrong thing you did cannot jeopardize your relationship with God. You do not need to fear his punishment but can instead pray to him right now and enjoy his lovingkindness as you confess your sin. He has even promised that the harm your sin has caused others will eventually be made right too. And he will give you the courage you need to apologize to them for what you did wrong.

Did someone wrong you? Have you been hurt by a person's words or actions? We all know what that is like and how awful it feels, especially when the harm comes from a friend or a loved one, but the good news is Jesus is going to hold everyone accountable for everything they have done wrong, including that person who has hurt you. Furthermore, God has promised that you will progressively and ultimately be healed from that harm by Jesus himself.

Did that bad habit get the best of you this past weekend? Are you in the spiral of addiction to something? I know exactly what that hopeless feeling is like. The powerlessness of it is absolutely agonizing, but the good news is Jesus is really the Lord who reigns over the most tempting sin that exists. You can go to him right now in prayer to get more power so that you experience less of that compulsion, and he has guaranteed us that we will one day live forever without any temptation whatsoever. Our future beyond death is one where we will never again be burdened by the guilt and shame associated with not being able to control ourselves.

What bad things are happening in your life? Are you fighting an illness? Or watching a loved one succumb to a disease? Are you in a conflict that feels like it will never be resolved? Is your body breaking down or beset with a disability? Did something tragic strike your family? Have you recently stood over a grave with the remains of someone very important to you?

No matter what you are experiencing today or what you experience every day for the rest of your earthly life, Lord–Sin–Savior–Faith is always good news. Perhaps Jesus summed up the application of this truth best when he said:

> **'In the world you will have tribulation. But take heart; I have overcome the world.' John 16:33**

The human experience in this world invariably involves temptation and regret, pain and suffering, failure and disappointment, deterioration and death. The bad news is truly bad, but there is a reason for encouragement in the face of it all. His name is Jesus. He is the Lord. He is putting the world right regarding sin. He is the only Savior of sinners. He is saving sinners by grace through faith. He has overcome the world and he is leading his followers into a brand-new world. This message about Jesus is good every day.

I truly hope that I have convinced you that the Gospel is always good news, but I also need to point out that it's only good every day if we get it right, right? Fake news about Jesus isn't helpful at all. More than that, false reporting about him is harmful. Truth and accuracy are very important for the good news to be truly good. Be sure to read the next chapter in order to understand why we must get the Gospel right in our minds and why it is vital to focus on keeping it right in our minds every day. Otherwise, it won't always be good news to us.

6

Why We Must Get
the Gospel Right

✳   ✳   ✳

TRUTH and accuracy is the first and most important tenet of the five tenets of journalism. It is the cardinal principle, and for good reason. There's the obvious ethical matter related to the very definition of journalism itself. Journalism is the profession that discovers and distributes the facts about events and people. Reporters report on realities. They explain what happened as best they can understand it. Without truth and accuracy, journalism isn't really journalism. It's propaganda.

In addition, there's the business aspect of it. Truth and accuracy are foundational, not just to journalism, but to the long-term success of any commercial enterprise. In the case of the news, correspondents who report inaccurate stories lose credibility for themselves and their companies. Fewer people trust them as a source of news and the company loses money. If it happens too often, those types of correspondents are fired and the companies that tolerate them eventually shut down.

Truth and accuracy are important in terms of journalistic ethics and business, but perhaps they are most important because inaccuracy can be harmful. In 2021, the mobile communications company T-Mobile released a lighthearted advertisement highlighting the negative results of inaccurate communication.

When discussing what to wear to an evening social gathering for work colleagues, one woman says to another on the cell phone, 'Just wear something not too crazy. Remember, it's a business dinner, not a costume party.' Due to the shoddy reception of that mobile company's network, all the other woman hears is, 'Just wear something crazy. Remember, it's a costume party.' To her embarrassment, she shows up to the business dinner in a fancy Renaissance style dress complete with extravagant regalia on her head. Inaccurate reporting can have negative effects like that. In fact, the consequences can be much less humorous. Falsehoods can be devastating.

Consider the ancient true story of Cleopatra and Marc Antony. On August 2, 30 b.c., Marc Antony received the bad news from a messenger that Cleopatra killed herself. In his grief over the loss of his one true love, he stabbed himself with his sword, only to find out shortly thereafter from another messenger that she was, in fact, still alive. He had his servants carry him in haste to see her, but it was too late. He died in her arms. Distraught, she killed herself a couple weeks later. Their tragic love story, made famous in our time by Shakespeare's play, is a good example of why news that is false or even somewhat inaccurate can be harmful. For them, it was a matter of life and death.

Since the Apostle Paul was a Roman citizen who lived just a generation after Cleopatra and Marc Antony, he very likely knew their story. And there's no doubt that Paul shared the values of truth and accuracy that modern day journalists have today. He was particularly concerned about that when it came to Gospel reporting. That's why he warned the ancient church in Galatia so strongly about anyone who preached a false gospel. Look what he wrote in a letter to them:

'But even if we or an angel from heaven should preach to you a gospel contrary to the one we preached to you, let him be accursed. As we have said before, so now I say again: If anyone is preaching to you a gospel contrary to the one you received, let him be accursed.' Galatians 1:8-9

This is a very strong warning, as strong as it gets. The Apostle Paul thought that people who preached a false gospel deserved much worse than getting fired from their job or shutting down their news agency. They deserved to be accursed. What does that mean?

When we use some form of the word 'curse,' we often simply mean that we want something bad to happen to that person like, 'Curse them!' That's the most common way it is used, but Paul clearly had something more theologically significant in mind. It warrants a bit of explanation.

Later in this same letter to the Galatian church, Paul described all Christians as the opposite of accursed. He referred to them as blessed. All Christians are blessed, not cursed, according to Paul, because Jesus became a curse for us on the Cross to redeem us from the curse caused by sin. We were cursed, but we put our faith in Jesus and thus became blessed. That's part of the good news about him.

Given that context, it seems clear that Paul thought people who preach a false gospel should be considered as still under the curse of sin. In other words, by preaching a different good news they proved that they were not Christians. True Christians preach the Gospel delivered once for all from Jesus to the church through the Apostles, which I have articulated under the headlines Lord, Sin, Savior, and Faith.

People who preach a different gospel aren't Christians because their gospel has no means by which to remove the curse caused by sin. Jesus is the only Savior of sinners. Salvation from curse unto blessing is found in no one else. There's no other name under Heaven by which people can be saved. Thus, people who change the Gospel to something contrary to it, remain cursed.

Further, there was a sense that Paul wanted the church in Galatia to avoid these false preachers. The leaders of the church should keep them out of the church and consider them as not part of the church. The Greek root word of accursed is anathema. Throughout church history, to be anathema has meant that you were excommunicated from the fellowship of the church. The origin of that meaning and practice is Paul's letter to the Galatians. That's an additional aspect of what he meant by 'let him be accursed.'

And the final implication is that those who preach a false gospel are in danger of Hell. Though some readers, pastors and scholars have attempted to avoid the gravity of the language in these verses, I don't see any way around understanding it as Paul pronouncing eternal condemnation on people who continue to get the Gospel wrong. 'Let him be accursed' is another way to say that what he is doing warrants damnation by God himself.

According to Paul, that 'gospel' reporter doesn't merely need to be fired. That 'good news' agency doesn't simply need to be shut down. If they keep up that practice for the rest of their lives, they deserve everlasting punishment from God himself.

Why would Paul use such strong language? Why such a severe statement? Well, it makes perfect sense when you think about it. Proclaiming the good news about Jesus is a joyful matter, but it is also a gravely serious one that requires truth and accuracy.

In the case of the news about Cleopatra, it turned out to be a matter of life and death for Marc Antony. The first messenger who told him the false news about Cleopatra was very likely put to death, especially if he did it intentionally. That punishment was just. It was right for him to suffer the same consequences that getting the news wrong wrought on Marc Antony.

In the case of the news about Jesus, it is more than a matter of life and death to whoever hears it. It is a matter of eternal life and endless death. If a Gospel messenger got it wrong and thus led people astray about the most important news in human history, the Apostle Paul thought that preacher should suffer the same consequences that their error wrought on others. Since getting the Gospel of Jesus right is ultimately a matter of Heaven or Hell for those who hear it, preaching the Gospel with truth and accuracy ought to be a matter of Heaven or Hell for those who preach it.

This was so important to the Apostle Paul that he wrote it twice in the beginning of his letter to the Galatians for clarity and emphasis. He didn't want to be vague on this topic. He didn't want anyone confused. And notice, he didn't just write it twice. Galatians 1:9 reads 'as we have already said.' That 'we' is a reference to the time when Paul and his Apostolic band of missionaries were actually in Galatia in person. They preached the good news about Jesus to the Galatians in A.D. 46 face-to-face.

It is likely that Paul looked these Galatians in the eye back then and told them that Jesus is the Lord who is putting the world right regarding sin, the only one who can do that, the only Savior of sinners. And he is saving sinners by grace through faith.

Then, he said something like, 'Even if I myself return next year and say to you, "I got it wrong the first time. The Gospel is different than what I first told you. It's not Lord, Sin, Savior, and Faith. I was mistaken." Don't believe me! May I be eternally condemned! Even if an angel comes down from Heaven and tells you that the angel who announced Jesus' birth to the shepherds in the night got it wrong and the new angel has the true gospel, don't believe the new angel. May that angel be accursed. No matter who it is, if that person preaches another gospel, may he burn in Hell.' The Apostle told them in person and then he wrote it twice in his epistle to the Galatians as a reminder.

It is important to understand, though, that Paul does not seem to be referring to a Christian who is talking about Jesus in everyday conversation and makes an unintentional mistake out of humble ignorance. He did not mean, 'Christian, if you make even the slightest mistake in your conversations about Jesus, may you be eternally condemned.' No, that's not what he meant.

Rather, he was referring to people who purposely perverted and twisted the Gospel. Paul wrote this letter to the Galatians because preachers and teachers from a theological school, a seminary of sorts, were doing just that. They visited Galatia and tried to convince the Galatian churches that their gospel was the right one and that the Gospel the Apostles handed down to the Galatians from Jesus himself was wrong. This was systematic, well thought out, intentional, false teaching.

Even so, the force of the language remains. It's jarring and uncomfortable to read, 'Let him be accursed.' It should be taken seriously by everyone, gravely so. The obvious application for us is that we must get the Gospel right. If you are a pastor like me, you have to tell the truth when you proclaim the good news. If you aren't a pastor, it's still important for you to be accurate. You as an individual and we as the church have to be clear about this message. There is no more important priority on planet Earth.

Given this warning in Galatians and the intense focus of the New Testament on the good news about Jesus, you would think that all Christians would be clear about what the Gospel actually is. You would think that there would be a consensus about it, a common definition. Yet, that is not what I experience and probably not what you experience either.

For example, we ask the question, 'What is the Gospel?' all the time at our church. We ask it when we speak to baptism candidates. We ask it in our church membership classes. We ask parents that question before child dedication. We ask it during our leadership training class. We ask it when we interview potential staff. We ask it a lot.

And in addition to all the asking that goes on at my church, I have personally asked that question to a wide variety of people, particularly over the last fifteen years. I have asked pastors, scholars, missionaries, and lay people. I have asked non-Christians, new Christians and 90-year-old church lifers. I have asked children, teenagers, and adults. I have asked my own children to the point that they are probably tired of being asked. I have asked that question a lot.

After all this asking, I have come to one clear conclusion. People are unclear about the content of the Gospel of Jesus. We just aren't quite sure what it is. Even the most well-educated Christians are not 100 percent confident about their understanding.

Here is the remarkably consistent pattern of behavior I observe when I ask people about the good news: They answer slowly and hesitantly. It takes them time and thought. It seems quite difficult. They often appear caught off guard by the question even when the context of the conversation makes it a natural question to ask. They search hard to find the right words and are surprised that the answer does not come quickly. Most folks are insecure about their answer being accurate.

Isn't that odd? Don't you find that strange? After all, the Gospel is the most basic and fundamental message of the Christian faith. It is Christianity 101. It seems like it should be a question that people answer quickly and easily, especially believers. Yet, it is difficult.

If I asked ten random Christians, I would very likely get ten different answers, many of which would be hesitantly expressed. If I asked you today and then asked you in a month, you might give me two different answers. And we may both wonder why it wasn't the same the last time you told me. Since you have just read this book, I would certainly wonder why you didn't simply use the headlines of the good news I have described: Lord, Sin, Savior, and Faith.

But, you definitely wouldn't be alone in vacillating between various understandings of the message. For example, there's a book being published in May 2023 called *5 Views on the Gospel* in Zondervan's Counterpoint Series. That series provides a forum for comparison and critique of different views on issues. The Christian publishing world openly acknowledges that we don't have clarity on the good news about Jesus!

The Apostle Paul told us that it is a matter of eternal life and endless death to get the Gospel right. Yet, we can't even come to agreement about a definition of it. I'm not sure I can contribute more than what I have written up to this point in this book to help in achieving a consensus, but I do have some additional thoughts as to why we don't have one. If the Gospel hasn't been clear to you up to this point in your life, the next chapter provides four reasons that may have been true.

7

Why the Gospel Can
Be Unclear

✳   ✳   ✳

WHEN I was in my forties, I vividly remember the sudden onset of farsightedness – words on a page being blurry the closer they got to my eyes. It was so discouraging, not just because it happened so quickly, but also because I was already nearsighted. Since middle school, I have worn glasses because I couldn't see things clearly that were far away. Then, as I entered middle age, those very same glasses that helped me see better weren't helpful at all when it came to reading my Bible in bed. In fact, they made it worse. So, I went to my eye doctor, and he explained how common this was, why it happened, and how I could address it. And my discouragement quickly faded.

I want to diminish your discouragement about not seeing the Gospel clearly if that has been the case with you. Just like that doctor did for me, I want to provide you some comfort as to why you may have lacked confidence in defining the good news. There are very good reasons why it may not have been clear to you. In fact, it is probably less about you than you might think.

In other words, if you have had trouble keeping the Gospel clear in your mind, I don't think it is because you aren't smart enough to understand it. It's not about your IQ. Furthermore, I doubt you struggle to articulate it because you are incompetent regarding spiritual things. I'm guessing you're probably not a wickedly immoral person. And I can't imagine that your lack of clarity comes from a lack of interest. You are reading a book on it after all.

Why is it so hard to define the Gospel? Why might you be uncertain about its content even after just reading this content that I have written? Why isn't there widespread agreement about it in the Christian world? Here are four answers to that question. I hope they reduce your own insecurity about not having a good handle on the good news.

First, the Gospel is simple and deep at the same time. It is a straightforward, easy, and uncomplicated message. Yet, it is also dense, unfathomable, and profound. I explained the Gospel to all four of my children when they were young, and they readily understood it. However, I also produced a doctoral project of 100,000+ words that still hasn't even come close to exploring all the depths of its meaning and application.

In that way, the Gospel is like the ocean or the universe. A child knows the joy of sandcastles at the beach with the calming sound of the waves, but the world's most knowledgeable and experienced oceanographers would never say they truly know all that the ocean is. Likewise, most people know the wonder of looking up at a dark night sky filled with bright stars and a full moon, but would any astronomer ever proclaim to understand the cosmos?

How do you define the ocean? How do you sum it up in a way that is faithful to its depths? How about the universe? What can one succinctly say to describe it in all its immensity? Though both ocean and universe are easy to experience, they are also quite overwhelming and, thus, difficult to define. I think that simple, but deep aspect also makes the Gospel hard to keep straight in our mind.

Even as you read the headlines of the good news in this book, I suspect it was hard for you not to get a bit lost in the depths of the message. That's why, at the end of each chapter, I attempted to pull you back up from those depths to the simple main points of it. That's first. The Gospel is simple and deep. That may be why it has been unclear to you.

Second, the Gospel is not regularly emphasized in our churches. Admittedly, I do not have hard data on this statement. And I don't mean to denigrate the church. That's not my intention. It is simply my observation that many churches do not consistently preach the Gospel.

Some of those churches don't hold the Bible in very high regard. They believe it is merely man's word about God, not God's definitive Word to humanity. The result of that worldview is they don't feel compelled to preach the Gospel of the Scriptures. They don't emphasize it because they have little motivation to know it or believe it. They don't think it's that much more important than their own thoughts about what constitutes good news from God. So, of course, their congregations are unclear about what the Gospel is.

Other churches know it and believe it, but think it is primarily a message for non-Christians. They only preach the Gospel for outreach events or during worship services when they think more unbelievers will be there. They don't regularly proclaim it because they aren't convinced it is a message for Christians too. Instead, they focus their teaching on how believers should live their lives. Therefore, their congregations can also be prone to being unsure about the content of the Gospel. Perhaps you attend a church like one of these two examples. That could be a second reason why it's been unclear.

Third, the human heart drifts from the Gospel. Even if you attend a church that does emphasize it, another challenge to certainty about the good news is that your humanity does not help you in your effort. I imagine you are like me. When my feet hit the ground in the morning, I'm usually thinking about all that I need to get done today or maybe how much I don't want to do what I know I must do. I am not thinking about what God has done, is doing, and will do in Jesus. I am not inherently motivated to contemplate the Gospel.

Furthermore, there is a tide in my very nature that is consistently pushing against me thinking clearly about it. I'm bent away from clarity on it. The sea provides a helpful analogy. In college after a doubleheader in Panama City, Florida, my baseball teammates and I swam straight out into the Gulf of Mexico to reach a sandbar, but we never quite got there. When we returned to shore sometime later, we found ourselves one-quarter of a mile away from where we left and exhausted. Unbeknownst to us, the tide was pushing us back to shore and East.

It's a bit like that with our fallen human nature. We drift away from God not towards God. It is a regular battle to maintain clarity about the message of Jesus. It is like swimming against the tide. You are in that battle every day. It is certainly one reason why you may struggle to keep the Gospel clear in your mind.

Lastly, the Bible is not a dictionary. It is not like you can simply turn to the 'G' section signified by a tab sticking out of the book and get the definition of the Gospel. It is much harder than that.

And if you look up Gospel in the table of contents, you may be slightly misled as to its meaning because Matthew, Mark, Luke, and John are sometimes called gospels, even though these books aren't entitled 'gospel' in the original language, nor are they limited to the Gospel in their content. They are theologized biographies of Jesus of Nazareth, not good news lexicons.

The Bible is a collection of sixty-six books written by about forty authors over 1500 years in fifteen+ genres. Determining the meaning of a word used in this vast and diverse book requires more than scanning the table of contents or doing a quick search. It warrants studying all the occurrences of that word, its cognates, and its idioms across all that material, each in its context.

If you do that, you will find that the Bible doesn't contain one, explicit, repeated definition of the good news. Though most of the information on the Gospel is in the New Testament, even there it isn't easy to quickly identify. The Apostles explained it in different ways without contradicting each other. Synthesizing their views into one concise definition faithful to all the Bible teaches about the Gospel is quite a difficult task – very hard indeed.

Furthermore, when you do that kind of research you will also discover that the Gospel is an eternal message that is progressively revealed, both in the Bible and in history. This dynamic may present the most significant challenge of all. It is not as simple as just taking the last 'definition' we see in Scripture. We need to take great care that the last revelation is also informed by all the previous revelations of it and that we are identifying the difference between the headlines of the good news and the depth of the details about it.

All the occurrences of the message in the Bible have consistency since they are the same message. At the same time, some of those occurrences are more well-developed and each one is contextualized to the situation and the specific time-period of salvation history. That makes it extremely difficult to define. It could be why you have had some trouble.

Is your head spinning even more right now? It is not hard to understand why. The Gospel is simple and deep. It's not regularly emphasized in our churches. Our hearts drift from it. And the Bible isn't a dictionary that provides a direct definition of it. If you have had difficulty maintaining clarity about the message of Jesus, there are at least these four solid reasons for that. There may be others.

That's one reason I wrote this book. To make the Gospel clear to you. It is the burden of my life to make it as clear to as many people as possible. I hope you use those four headlines about Jesus – Lord, Sin, Savior and Faith – as a tool to keep it clear. And I hope you share it with others often. As you may have already concluded, there is an urgency to do so.

8

Why We Must Share
the Good News

✳ ✳ ✳

CARINGBRIDGE is a non-profit organization dedicated to making sure no one in the world has to go through health challenges without support. It was started in 1997 by Sona Mehring when one of her friends gave birth to a child prematurely. That baby girl faced all sorts of health challenges and her family and friends wanted to know what was happening. With a heart full of compassion, Sona created a website to keep everybody regularly up to date on the situation. It relieved the stress of communication from the child's parents while also enabling everyone else to support them in various ways.

As it is with most pastors, I always seem to be following a CaringBridge website for someone we know. They are so helpful as they direct my prayers in such specific ways, but they are also quite agonizing at times. We have several beloved church members who are currently battling Stage IV cancer. Reading those particular updates is an emotional roller coaster with a lot of bad news. I often pray for comfort and perseverance, but I am not shy about pleading with God for more, wanting desperately that these folks would experience the miracle of complete healing. What good news it would be for them to hear a doctor say, 'We can't totally explain this, but the cancer is gone!' I'm sure you have prayed the same prayer for someone you know.

Now, imagine you were a researcher in the field of oncology and one day in the lab, you and your colleagues discovered a cure for the very cancer that was ravaging the body of a friend for whom you were praying that exact prayer. You tested it multiple times and it worked every time. What would you do?

Wouldn't you immediately call that friend to tell them the good news? Wouldn't you post a response that very day on their CaringBridge website celebrating the fact that you have the cure and are rushing over to administer it? Wouldn't you tell the world so that anyone suffering from that particular cancer would have the hope of receiving this new medication? If you had the cure for a deadly disease, would you keep it to yourself? Of course, you wouldn't. No one would. There's an urgency to share the cure because people are suffering and need to hear the good news that their misery can end if they would simply receive it.

So, let me ask you, why would you keep the good news about Jesus to yourself? The Gospel is to sin as a cure is to cancer. And there are people you know and love who are right at this very moment suffering in their personal sin. They are ashamed about what they have done wrong. Their guilt is eating them up inside. Deep down, they know the truth that their sins deserve God's judgment, and they are living in a quiet misery of the soul under the fear of his wrath.

Your family and friends need someone to tell them the good news that Jesus is the Christ. He is righting every wrong they have ever done in such a way that they can be forgiven for all of it. He is the only one who can do that, and he will do it by grace through their faith. They simply need to trust him. It is urgent that you share the Gospel with them so that they can experience the joy of being saved from the penalty of their sin. If you won't, who will?

Why would you keep the good news about Jesus to yourself? There are people living in your neighborhood who are suffering under the dominion of indwelling sin. Behind the closed doors of their house, it is oppressing them and always getting the best of them. They have a desire to do the right thing but cannot consistently say no to the temptation to do wrong. They are living in the miserable cycle of trying to earn God's favor by what they do, but regularly find themselves doing what they know in their heart displeases him.

Your neighbors need someone to tell them the good news that Jesus is the King. He is righting all that is wrong within human beings in such a way that they can receive power to change. He is the only one who can truly set them free from the grip of sin, and he will do it by grace through their faith. They just need to rely on him. It is urgent that you tell them this message so that they can feel the peace of being delivered from the power of their sin. If you don't, who will?

Why would you keep the good news about Jesus to yourself? There are people where you work and where you play, where you socialize and where you rest, where you shop and where you study, and even where you worship, who are struggling to cope with effects of original sin. The mess in their life has frayed their nerves. The deterioration of their body is depressing their soul. The failures of their past are troubling their mind. Their weaknesses are immobilizing their wills. The conflict in their home has made them feel homeless. The chemotherapy has worn them out. And the death around them has led them to despair of life itself.

There are people everywhere you go who need to hear that Jesus is the Son of God who is going to put the entire world right in such a way that they can be resurrected into a New Heaven and a New Earth. He is the only Savior of sinners, and he will save us by grace. The only condition for that salvation is faith in him. It is urgent that you explain the good news to them so that their hearts are filled with hope. As the Apostle Paul pleaded with the ancient church in Rome, I plead with you:

> **'How are they to believe in him of whom they have never heard? And how are they to hear without someone preaching?'**
> **Romans 10:14**

How will your friends, family, neighbors, coworkers, etc., put their faith in Jesus without you telling them the good news about him? Why not speak to them today about him? Why not share the four headlines of Lord, Sin, Savior, and Faith? Why not give them a copy of this book? Why not invite them to discuss it with you?

You know how good the Gospel is for you every single day, how you need to be reminded of it for the good of your own soul. So, why not make that call? Why not start that conversation? Why not set that appointment? Don't let fear of rejection stop you. Don't let your insecurity hold you back. Don't let other priorities in your life crowd out God's most important priority on Earth. Don't let anything get in your way.

Do you really believe that the Gospel is always good news? Then, please recognize the urgency to share it with as many people as possible. You and I and every other Christian are the means by which God is announcing his message. We are the plan. People must hear it from us in order to believe it. The only way for them to be rescued from sin and its destructive consequences is to put their faith in Christ. I urge you to read what the Apostle Paul wrote in Romans 10:17 and act on it: '**So faith comes from hearing, and hearing through the word of Christ.**'

The word of Christ, the Gospel, is the power of God for salvation. The Lord uses you speaking this message to others to create faith in them. Without us preaching to them, how will they hear? Without them hearing about Jesus, how will they have faith in him? Without faith in him, how will they be saved? Let's love people enough to simply tell them about the love of God for them in Jesus Christ.

Now, as I conclude this book on the good news of Jesus with this exhortation about the urgency to share it, I don't want to disorient you, but I wonder if you have noticed that, though I used the word 'love' in that last sentence, it is not one of the four key words in my understanding of the message itself – Lord, Sin, Savior, and Faith. Perhaps you did. It is not hard to see that 'love' is not one of those words. It is not in the headlines.

Did you notice that I didn't even use 'love' at all in the way I sum up the Gospel in its simplest form? Read it again just so you are crystal clear about this. The Gospel is the good news about Jesus of Nazareth:

- Jesus is the Lord.

- Jesus is putting the world right regarding sin.

- Jesus is the only Savior of sinners.

- Jesus is saving sinners by grace through faith.

The word 'love' is not in the Gospel in the way that I have presented it. Did that occur to you as you read this book? And if it did, did you wonder why that is? I mean, how can that possibly be? Isn't the Gospel best described as 'God loves you?' Isn't John 3:16 the finest summary of the good news? Well, be sure to read the final chapter to learn how God's love relates to the message. You do not want to miss this final insight.

9

Why Love Isn't a Headline

∗   ∗   ∗

THE 20th century's most famous evangelist Billy Graham once said, 'This is the one Scripture that I always preach on in a crusade, usually on the opening night. I suppose it is the most familiar passage in the Bible. It has only twenty-five words in the English translation of it, but it is the Gospel in a nutshell.' What is the one Scripture he was referring to? It was John 3:16:

> **'For God so loved the world, that he gave his only Son, that whoever believes in him should not perish but have eternal life.'**

Like Dr. Graham, many people consider this verse to be the Gospel in a nutshell. That seemed to be Charles Spurgeon's view too. The 19th-century 'Prince of Preachers' said, 'I cannot preach from this text anything but a simple Gospel sermon.' Apparently, he felt constrained by the words of John 3:16 to stick to a basic good news message because the words of that verse so matched that message. Likewise, the 16th-century reformer Martin Luther once referred to John 3:16 as 'The Gospel in Miniature,' describing it as the very heart of the Bible and the message of Jesus Christ.

If John 3:16 has come to your mind when you have thought about the good news of Jesus, you are not only in the majority, but you are also in really good company. Graham, Spurgeon, and Luther are not a bad endorsement list.

Why then, is it not in this book until this chapter? Am I just being provocative? Contrarian? Or worse, heretical? Well, I'd strongly prefer to be none of those. I'm simply seeking to define the Gospel in the most Biblically faithful way possible. And, several years ago, I stumbled across a stunning and disorienting bit of biblical data that changed my understanding of the headlines of the good news and caused me to rethink it, particularly the use of the word 'love' in articulating it.

Reflect on that bit of biblical data now. It is found in a single verse embedded in the first Apostolic council's letter to Gentile believers about the life that accords with the Gospel:

> 'It has seemed good to us, having come to one accord, to choose men and send them to you with our <u>beloved</u> Barnabas and Paul.' Acts 15:25

Now, at first glance, this verse seems fairly ordinary and even unrelated to the definition of the Gospel. What is so stunning about it to me? What is so disorienting that it would cause me to rethink the headlines of the good news, particularly the use of the word 'love' in articulating it?

Well, this word 'beloved' in Acts 15:25 is the only occurrence of the word 'love' in the entire book of Acts. You might want to read that sentence over again to soak it in. Or perhaps I should simply repeat it. This word 'beloved' in Acts 15:25 is the only occurrence of the word 'love' in the entire book of Acts.

In other words, it is not simply that the word 'love' is absent from the book, but rather that there is not even a cognate of the word 'love' to be found anywhere. That is, the words 'loved,' 'loves,' 'loving,' 'lover,' and 'lovely' are all absent too. Basically, there's no 'love' in Acts!

That's a stunning bit of data. I still find it hard to process. Sometimes I still don't believe it. I want to get back on my computer Bible search tool and redo my research to see if it is really true. You might be thinking of doing that yourself right now.

Why do I find it so hard to believe? Why is it so disorienting? Consider that Acts is the historical record of the evangelistic activity of the Apostles. It is the God-inspired account of the Gospel going forward to the entire Roman Empire. It is the only New Testament narrative that describes the content and nature of the Spirit-filled, Gospel-preaching ministry of men like Peter, Paul, and Philip, men after whom the church patterns our Gospel preaching.

As such, it contains direct quotes from their lips as well as summary descriptions of their sermons to non-Christians. It seems quite strange, then, doesn't it, especially for those of us who have long understood the Gospel to begin with 'God loves you' that the word 'love' is not found anywhere in the book of Acts.

Nowhere does Luke record, 'And Paul said to the crowd gathered in the town square, "God loves you," because he wanted them to understand the gospel.' Nowhere is it written, 'Peter told the Samarians how much God loved them in Jesus Christ.' Doesn't that strike you as odd? They are never recorded as reciting John 3:16.

How can it be that the Biblical book about the preaching of the Gospel in the world does not include the word 'love' when the whole world seems to understand the Gospel as 'God so loved the world ...'? How are we to process that 'love' is not in Acts? What does that mean for the definition of the Gospel and the use of the word 'love' in it?

Well, here's what I have concluded. While the Bible makes it clear that God is love and that God loves everyone, the Apostles didn't use the word 'love' when they preached the Gospel as recorded in Acts because 'God loves you' is a very general statement. It is not specific enough about Jesus of Nazareth. And they wanted to be clear about the message. Nothing was more important to them.

So, although 'God loves you' is a good word to share with anyone you meet, it is not how the Bible describes communicating the good news. Perhaps think about it this way. It's a bit of a paradox. The very best way to tell someone who doesn't know about God that God loves them is not by simply saying to them, 'God loves you.' That message is left wide open to their understanding of God, themselves, and love.

The very best way to tell someone that God loves them is by telling them the good news about Jesus of Nazareth. When they hear the Gospel, they learn about the astounding love of God in Jesus. It is defined for them from God's perspective:

- Jesus is the Lord.
- Jesus is putting the world right regarding sin.
- Jesus is the only Savior of sinners.
- Jesus is saving sinners by grace through faith.

That is the ultimate expression of God's love for the world. That is the Gospel of Jesus. And it's always good news.